Ordnance Survey

# LONDON

## CITY WALKS

### Compiled by
### Andy Rashleigh

Andy Rashleigh is a Blue Badge Guide, qualified City Guide and member of the Guild of Registered Tour Guides.

# Contents

| Introduction to City Walks London | | page 4 | |
|---|---|---|---|
| **Walks** | | **Start** | **Finish** |
| 1 | Money, Money, Money<br>**The Square Mile** | Bank | Bank |
| 2 | Pepys, Plague and Fire<br>**The City of London** | Monument | Tower Hill |
| 3 | That Most Fractious Hamlet in the Tower Division<br>**Spitalfields** | Liverpool Street Station | Liverpool Street Station |
| 4 | To the Banks of the Fleet<br>**Smithfield** | St Paul's | Farringdon |
| 5 | Monks, Nuns and the Dispossessed<br>**Clerkenwell** | Farringdon | The Angel |
| 6 | The Liberty of the Bishop of Winchester<br>**The South Bank** | Embankment | London Bridge |
| 7 | The Judge and the Showgirl<br>**Holborn and Covent Garden** | Holborn | Covent Garden |
| 8 | The Duke of Bedford's Back Garden<br>**Bloomsbury** | Euston Square | Russell Square |
| 9 | For Parliament?<br>**Whitehall** | Charing Cross | Westminster |
| 10 | Or for the King?<br>**St James's** | Westminster | Green Park |
| 11 | We Never Closed<br>**Soho** | Tottenham Court Road | Piccadilly Circus |
| 12 | Only £400 on the Monopoly Board<br>**Mayfair** | Green Park | Green Park |
| 13 | A Park for All Seasons<br>**Hyde Park** | Marble Arch | High Street Kensington |
| 14 | In the Footsteps of the Sloane Ranger<br>**Chelsea** | Knightsbridge | Sloane Square |
| 15 | Turn Again Whittington<br>**Highgate** | Highgate | Archway |

| Tales for the telling en route | Page |
|---|---|
| The rise of the coffee house, the home of banking, modern architectural wonders, the Worshipful Company of Drapers, and the naughty nuns of St Helen's, Bishopsgate. | 6 |
| Two calamitous disasters, the Great Plague and Great Fire, destroyed medieval London but heralded much of the City we see today. | 12 |
| Jack the Ripper and the founding of Methodism bookend tales of the 'rag trade' from Belgian Huguenot weavers, through Jewish tailors to Bangladeshi textiles and fine food. | 18 |
| The patron saint of travellers; London's oldest hospital, tournaments, medieval executions, a 'bull in a china shop', and Bartholomew Fair with its rogue traders and Piepowder Court. | 24 |
| 18th-century gin distilling, the history of the St John Ambulance Association, a rallying point for marches on the capital, and the most unexpected Grade 1 listed building. | 30 |
| A riverside walk along the Thames tideway. Modern performance art to Shakespearian drama; from bear baiting to London's oldest market and glorious views across the water most of the way. | 36 |
| London's largest square, the Inns of Court and the Royal Courts of Justice are the precursor to a very British cup of tea courtesy of Twinings, then curtain up on a tour of Theatreland. | 42 |
| Poets, painters, novelists, education, Great Ormond Street Hospital for Sick Children and the British Museum, through the squares and gardens of the Bedford estate. | 48 |
| Whitehall and the 'Corridors of Power' from Trafalgar Square: Horse Guards Parade and the Household Cavalry, Downing Street, the Cenotaph, the Palace of Westminster and Big Ben. | 54 |
| St James's Park is the centrepiece of this walk but there are also two Royal Palaces, several grand houses, commemorative statues and the world of prestigious gentlemen's clubs in Pall Mall. | 60 |
| Fine dining and coffee bars, private members' clubs, adult entertainment, the home of 'Swinging London' as well as the GP who discovered the cause of cholera, and never far from thriving Chinatown. | 66 |
| Celebrated grocers, bespoke tailors and plush hotels, magnificent squares lined with plane trees and dotted with embassies ending at Shepherd Market, the site of the original May Fairs. | 72 |
| Echoes of duels past and highwaymen hanged on Tyburn Tree amid the sounds of present day recreation; memorial gardens, lakes and monuments, concluding at London's most expensive address. | 78 |
| High fashion, trendy shops and the home of the Young British Artists meet the traditional scarlet coats of the Chelsea Pensioners and England's earliest rockery in the Physic Garden. | 84 |
| A rarely sung verse in the National Anthem, an unfathomable drinking ritual, a narrow escape for Queen Victoria, philanthropists aplenty and tombs of the famous in the West and East Cemeteries. | 90 |

# Introduction to City Walks London

In using this book you have chosen to explore London in the best possible way - on foot. The sights, sounds and smells of the modern city can't disguise two millennia of extraordinary, rumbustious or, by turns, glorious and catastrophic history.

These walks take in the well-known sights – Westminster Abbey, Trafalgar Square, the Tower of London, but deliberately encourage you away from the well-beaten tourist track. Silk weavers in Spitalfields, the Bloomsbury Set and Jimi Hendrix are all part of London's story, as are Borough Market, Brick Lane and Carnaby Street. Discover the Christian church that became a synagogue and is now a mosque; see where Vladimir Lenin dispatched his

The Globe Theatre and Tate Modern, walk 6

The Jamaica Wine House, walk 1

so. Unlike many towns, counties or cities there is no parochial insistence that the only true citizen is the one who was born here – Stratford's Shakespeare, Germany's Karl Marx and the Californian Dennis Severs were all Londoners. While you remain in town, so are you. Be proud of your city and enjoy all it has to offer.

revolutionary tracts to Tsarist Russia; find out where the Prince of Wales has his boots made; eat a Smithfield Breakfast, a dim sum lunch or drink the best coffee.

London was already cosmopolitan when the Romans built the first bridge across the Thames nearly two thousand years ago and it remains

The Albert Memorial, walk 13

Richard Trevithick, walk 8

Don't be shackled by what is pointed out. Look around you. Be distracted by anything else that takes your fancy. Route commentaries are deliberately wide ranging from 'need to know' information to anecdotes and the downright quirky and these walks provide a taster for further exploration. If that's so, dig deeper – book an expert Blue Badge Guide or join one of the varied 'London Walks'. And whatever you do, don't miss out on some of the finest galleries and museums in the world which are free to visit. Then there's theatre, cinema, comedy clubs, concerts and the ceremonial duties of the King's Guard…
So much to see and do!

MONEY, MONEY, MONEY

# The Square Mile

**WALK 1**

The City of London. Founded as a trading centre by the Romans: in area, street plan and international feel, little has changed in 2000 years. Now, it is Europe's financial capital and probably the wealthiest square mile on Earth. During the week it buzzes with the activities of workers from every corner of the world: at weekends you can have it to yourself.

| Start ⊖ | Finish ⊖ | Distance | Refreshments |
|---|---|---|---|
| Bank | Bank | 1 mile (1.7km) | The Old Doctor Butler's Head |

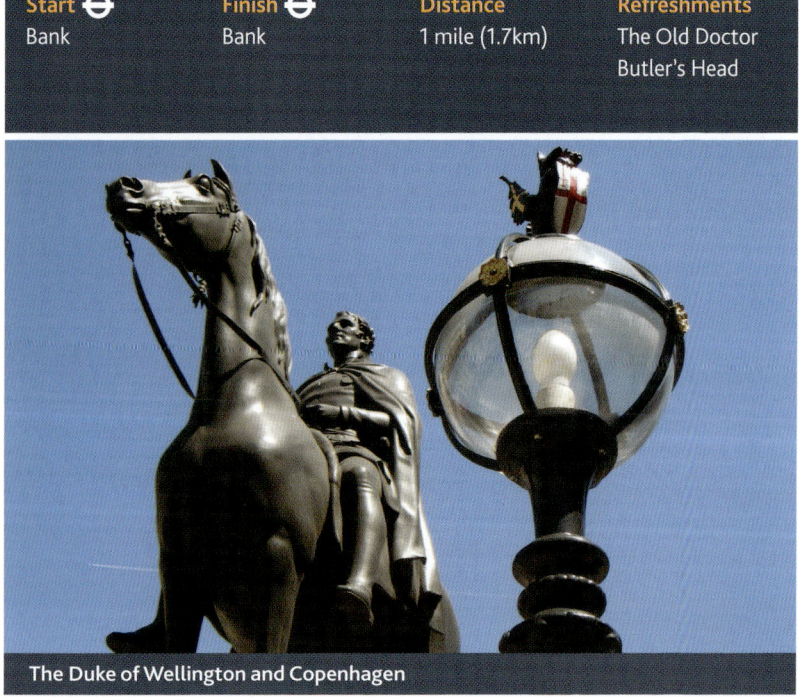

The Duke of Wellington and Copenhagen

## ON THIS WALK

- Royal Exchange
- Lombard Street
- Lloyd's of London
- Jamaica Wine House
- Leadenhall Market
- St Andrew Undershaft

6 / WALK 1 – THE SQUARE MILE

**Leave Bank station at exit 3.**

As you emerge from the station, the bold, brazen colonnade of the Royal Exchange – in its third incarnation – looms above you. Take time to stand on the steps and look around. These steps are one of the places in London where a new monarch will be proclaimed.

The South African mining engineer, **James Greathead**, studies his map in the middle of Cornhill. In the 1860s his state of the art tunnelling shield was integral to construction of the underground system, and more recently, the Channel Tunnel and Crossrail.

Look across the road junction to the delicate classical columns of the **Mansion House**, home of the multi-tasking Lord Mayor of London, Admiral of the Port of London, Chief Magistrate, Head of the City of London Police who spends much of the year in office travelling the world to drum up business for The City. There has been a mayor since 1189: 26 years later Magna Carta enshrined the right of Londoners to elect who governs them. He, occasionally she, is elected by The Livery Companies and can only be outranked within The City by the reigning monarch.

To the right, the great curtain wall of the **Bank of England**. It is the Government's banker and, since the 18th century also to the high street clearing banks. The Bank has had a monopoly on the issue of banknotes in England and Wales since the early 20th century, but it is only since 1997 that its duties include responsibility for setting the UK's official interest rate. As well as providing banking services to its customers, the Bank of England manages the UK's foreign exchange and gold reserves. The curtain wall was built by Sir John Soane in response to the anti-Catholic riots led by Lord George Gordon in 1780. The central part dates from the 1920s when Soane's bank was found to be too small. If you're lucky enough to have an old-style £50 note (issued prior to November 2011 and withdrawn from circulation in 2014) you will see the portrait of the first governor, John Houblon, on its reverse side.

**Walk through the Royal Exchange if it's open, if closed continue along Cornhill.**

Since 2001 most insurance companies have departed and the Exchange now contains high-class shops and a café. Behind it, note the seated statue of the American philanthropist George Peabody, whose Peabody Homes all around London still provide accommodation for low paid workers in this most expensive of cities. Then the block of stone – a herm – with the head of Paul Julius Reuter whose news agency was originally based here until it moved to Fleet Street and thence to Canary Wharf. Look high above you and the statue is that of its founder, Sir Thomas Gresham, above him the family symbol, a grasshopper weathervane. A wealthy Elizabethan businessman, ambassador

| The Gherkin | Tower 42 | The Bank of England Museum |
|---|---|---|
| | St Helen's Church | Drapers Hall | Duke of Wellington |

WALK 1 – THE SQUARE MILE

and spy, while in Antwerp buying gunpowder for the Queen, Gresham saw that merchants conducted their business in a cloistered square called a bourse. In the 1560s he built the original exchange here, Queen Elizabeth requested that it be called the Royal Exchange. Legend has it that Sir Thomas crushed a pearl worth £1,500 in a goblet of wine and drank her health.

The drinking water fountain may remind you that this is where Renée Zellweger found Colin Firth in the snow at the end of the first 'Bridget Jones' film.

## Cross Cornhill and continue to St Michael's Church on the right.

Here is the maze of alleys in which Ebenezer Scrooge had his counting house: the bell that chimed the hour to herald each ghost was the bell of St Michael's, Cornhill. On Christmas Eve, Bob Cratchit left for his begrudged Christmas Day off and joyfully slid along the ice on Cornhill.

## Dive down St Michael's Alley to the right of the church.

On your left, the **Jamaica Wine House**. See how the step has been worn away by a hundred years' worth of barrels being rolled across it. And there's a blue plaque. You are at the sign of **Pasqua Rosee's Head**, London's first coffee house. Pasqua Rosee was servant to Daniel Webster, a merchant, who traded with Turkey and happened to make the best coffee in London. Webster got fed up with friends and colleagues dropping in 'by chance', so in 1652 he set Pasqua up with a coffee house. The passion for coffee was such that within 10 years there were 200 coffee houses in London. Each one developed its own identity: they became the main places to do business; the patrons of this particular house were involved in the West Indies trade. Coffee Houses encouraged educated men to debate the issues of the day and when Charles II was restored to the throne in 1660 he feared them as 'Universities of Sedition', suggested closing them down but, remembering what happened to his father, decided not to.

## Go straight past the 'George and Vulture' and down to Lombard Street.

The **George and Vulture** features in Charles Dickens' 'Pickwick Papers' as the refuge for Mr Pickwick while he's being sued for breach of promise by his landlady Mrs Bardell. In the 18 century it was the meeting place for the Hellfire Club, a society of rakes who would plan their less than savoury activities here. It is a chop house: beer and a chop was once the regular lunch of many city gents; times have changed but it can still be full to bursting at lunchtime.

**Lombard Street** is the home of banking. Lombard bankers were licensed to lend money by the Pope and they based themselves here, each one trading from a bench or 'banca'. Old individual bank signs still hang above the street.

## Head left down Lombard Street and left up Gracechurch Street.

**The Crosse Keys** pub on the left is the beautifully preserved Hong Kong and Shanghai Bank. They also serve coffee, if you need mid-jaunt refreshment!

## Cross the road and enter Leadenhall Market.

In 1377 there was a hall with a lead roof here and 'higglers' – pedlars from Essex

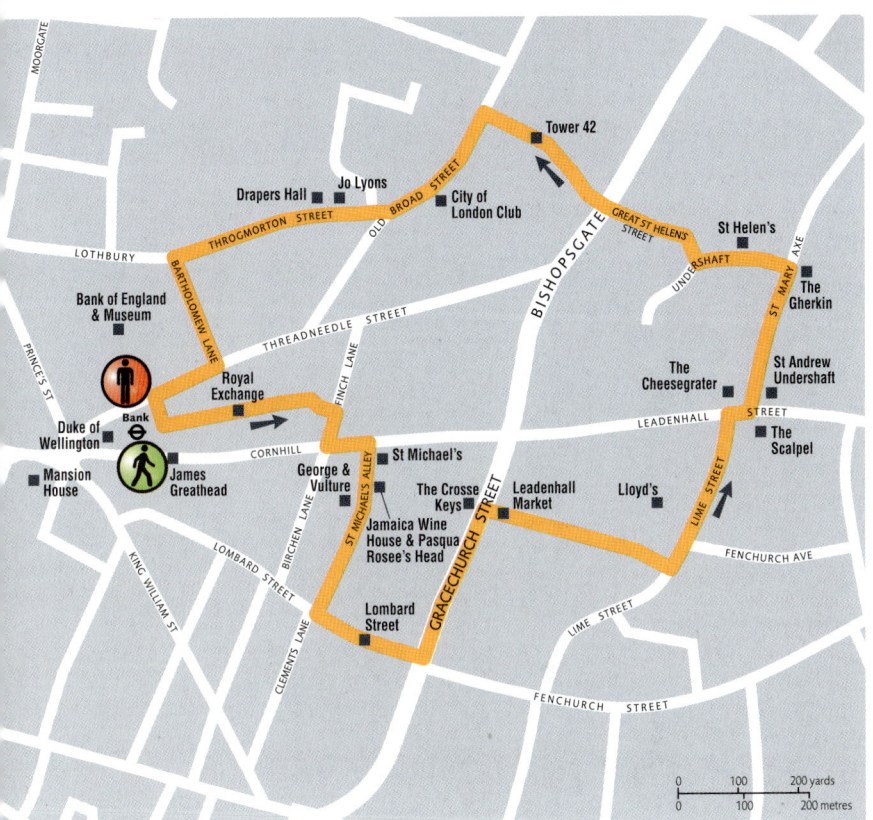

– were allowed to sell poultry, eggs, butter and cheese. Beneath us are the remains of the old Roman basilica: the present wrought iron, brightly painted Victorian arcade is the work of Horace Jones, of Tower Bridge fame. Now it is a retail centre, but explore the back alleys and you'll find Diagon Alley where Harry Potter bought his wand.

## Walk straight through the market.

On the left is **Lloyd's of London.** Created by Richard Rogers in 1988, this controversial structure divided opinion then as now. Rogers put all service facilities on the outside – staircases, lifts, kitchens and rest rooms – so that business can continue inside, uninterrupted by any necessary repair work on those facilities. A style known by some as 'bowellism'.

Lloyd's began life in Edward Lloyd's coffee house in Lombard Street in the 1680s. He sent a waiter to the Port of London each morning for reliable news of which ships were leaving or had arrived. It soon became the centre for marine insurance. Lloyd's still has the lion's share of high risk marine, aeronautical, mining and drilling contracts.

## Turn left down Lime Street.
Look to the right and there is the top heavy 'Walkie Talkie' with its 'Sky Garden' at the top. It is free to visit, but you need to book in advance. In the other direction is the **Gherkin**.

## Stop on the corner of Lime Street and Leadenhall Street.
The aptly named Cheesegrater is to the left. The rugby ball-shaped Gherkin

WALK 1 – THE SQUARE MILE / 9

is to the right and it looms above the medieval church of **St Andrew Undershaft**. The church is so named because a maypole towered over it until chopped up for firewood by Puritans in the 1500s. Now the church is occasionally referred to as St Andrew Undergherkin.

30 St Mary Axe, to use its correct title, opened in 2004 as the Swiss Re-Insurance headquarters. Designed by the architect Ken Shuttleworth for Norman Foster Associates it soon acquired the name 'The Gherkin' – a pickled dill cucumber. Acclaimed as 'London's first ecological tall building', the office space spirals round gardens of oxygenating vegetation and lighting and air-conditioning costs are profoundly lower than in a traditional building of its time. In a very few years this has become one of the most recognisable landmarks in The City.

At the same crossroads are the **Cheesegrater**, which opened in 2014, and the **Scalpel**, 2018, testament to the custom of giving buildings nicknames!

### Cross Leadenhall Street and at the base of the Gherkin turn left past the medieval church of St Helen, Bishopsgate.

St Helen's has survived fire, incendiaries and high explosive. It has an unusual double nave. The resident Benedictine nuns worshipped to the left and on the right, separated by a screen, the local parishioners. There were stern words when the Archbishop of Canterbury was informed that peepholes had been poked through the screen and nuns had been seen 'kissing secular persons and wearing ostentatious veils'. Even the Prioress was scolded for the number of little dogs she owned. In 1439 'dancing and revelling' were forbidden except at Christmas and then only among themselves!

### Bear right down Great St Helens to Bishopsgate past the Pinnacle. Cross Bishopsgate and into the alley, bearing right down the steps.

You are under the eaves of **Tower 42**. For years this was known as the Nat West Building, but the National Westminster Bank is now part of RBS and has fled elsewhere.

### Turn left down Old Broad Street.

On your left pass the Victorian **City of London Club** with its gas lamps and fruity canopy. Banquets, conferences and weddings right in the heart of The City.

### Fork right into Throgmorton Street past the Drapers' Hall.

The Worshipful Company of Drapers are third in order of precedence of London's Livery Companies. Until about 1650 nobody could start a business within the Square Mile unless they belonged to a Livery Company. They not only elected the Lord Mayor, but were immensely influential: in the Civil War (1640s) they backed Parliament against the King and that proved crucial. However, as London spread beyond the walls, their power might have waned, but their fortunes remain intact. In medieval times Livery Companies invested well, bought land and still collect rent on it. Now the companies use their resources to benefit education and charities.

Notice the doorway on the right which was the entrance to **Jo Lyons** from 1900. Was this a Lyons Corner

30 St Mary Axe - 'The Gherkin'

House with milky coffee, tea cakes and 'nippies'? Not at all, it once was the grandest and largest of all the Lyons restaurants.

As you emerge into Lothbury the back of the Bank of England greets you with a blank stare.

**Walk left down Bartholomew Lane with the Bank on your right.**

**The Bank of England Museum** is on the corner with Threadneedle Street and is free and fascinating. Along with a history of currency and the bank, see a reconstruction of Sir John Soane's original telling hall and find out whether you have the strength to lift a gold ingot.

**At the end of Bartholomew Lane turn right and cross over Threadneedle Street to where you started.**

Just one more thing. The mounted statue of the **Duke of Wellington** ahead of you dates from 1844. The victor of Waterloo sits on Copenhagen whose sire, Meteor, came second in the Derby in 1797. Like his father, Copenhagen was destined for the race track, but failed to shine and was sold to the army. He eventually died aged 35 and was given a funeral with full military honours at the Duke's country home of Stratfield Saye, Hampshire, where he is buried.

Go in any direction and you will find a plethora of cafés, restaurants and pubs. A favourite is The Old Doctor Butler's Head. Walk up Moorgate and left down Mason's Avenue. Cafés towards Moorgate.

WALK 1 – THE SQUARE MILE / 11

## PEPYS, PLAGUE AND FIRE

# The City of London

**WALK 2**

In 1660 after ten years of a buttoned-up puritan republic, Charles II was called back by parliament to be king. He and London let their hair down. Samuel Pepys' secret diary is the most indiscreet record we have of the next decade. But it wasn't all fun. The Great Plague and Great Fire of London in different ways destroyed the medieval city but heralded much of The City we know today.

| Start | Finish | Distance | Refreshments |
|---|---|---|---|
| Monument | Tower Hill | ¾ mile (1.3km) | The Hung, Drawn and Quartered |

The memorial to merchant seamen killed during The Falklands Conflict

## ON THIS WALK

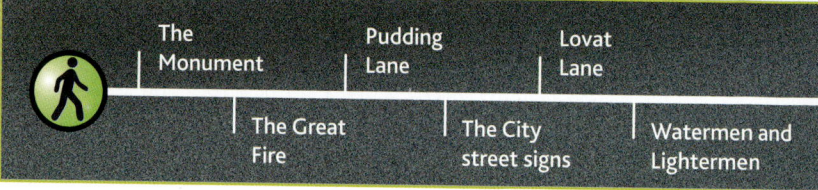

- The Monument
- Pudding Lane
- Lovat Lane
- The Great Fire
- The City street signs
- Watermen and Lightermen

WALK 2 – THE CITY OF LONDON

**Leave Monument station by the Fish Street Hill exit.**

Towering above you and crowned with a gilt bowl of flames is Christopher Wren's memorial to the Great Fire of London of 1666.

**The Monument** is 202 feet (61.5m) high, the exact distance from its base to the site in Pudding Lane where the fire began. It was for many years the tallest free standing column in the world. If you want to start your walk by climbing the 311 steps to the top, you will be given a certificate to hang on your wall.

The Great Fire began at 2.00am on Sunday 2nd September 1666 in the house of Thomas Farynor, a baker of ships' biscuits and meat pies for the navy.

It had been a hot dry August; the city built of wood was dry as a bone; all it required was a spark. There was a strong east wind that night: the fire spread with terrifying speed, feeding on the tar and pitch used to seal houses. Within an hour the Mayor, Sir Thomas Bloodworth, had been woken with the news. He was unimpressed, declaring that 'A woman might piss it out'.

By Thursday the fire was effectively extinguished, but only after destroying 13,200 houses, 84 churches and 44 company halls – 80% of The City. Did Londoners hold Thomas Farynor responsible? Not at all. Hysteria raged as fiercely as the flames, and fingers of blame pointed willy-nilly at all and any foreigners.

A slow-witted French watchmaker, Robert Hubert, confessed under torture to having deliberately started the fire at the bakery. The Earl of Clarendon commented that 'Neither the judges, nor any present at the trial did believe him guilty; but he was a poor distracted wretch, weary of his life, and chose to part with it'. He was hanged at Tyburn.

**Look carefully at the bas-relief on the western side of the column.**

Bottom left, the female figure representing London, clings on to her sword. Beneath her, a dragon with the shield of The City in its claws. Comforting 'London', winged Father Time indicates up to a cornucopia and olive branch of peace. The Roman soldier with the 17th-century full bottomed wig is King Charles II; he holds London's new charter and ushers Science, Architecture and Liberty to her aid. Behind him is brother James, Duke of York, whose finest hour this was as he led sailors of the Royal Navy in blowing up houses as firebreaks. Beneath them in a sewer, who on earth could that be but Envy? France? Holland? The Pope? Such was the straightforward propaganda of the time.

Until Catholic emancipation in 1831 at the base of The Monument were the words 'But Popish frenzy which wrought such horrors is not yet quenched.'

**Walk around the column and across the square past an inscription on the pavement for Robert Hooke, Wren's polymath friend and collaborator.**

At the foot of Pudding Lane is a **plaque**. A belated apology for the fire issued by the Bakers' Company in 1986. Well, better late than never.

## Part way up Pudding Lane take St George's Lane to the right.

Before you cross Botolph Lane, take a moment to study the distinctive, flamboyant **City of London street signs**. The coat of arms shows the cross of St George, with the sword of St Paul, London's patron saint, in its top left quadrant. The Latin motto can be translated as 'God Guide Us' and the two creatures supporting the shield are dragons. On every main road into The City there are dragons facing outwards to deter evil doers and protect Londoners.

## Cross Botolph Lane into Botolph Alley. At the end of the alley turn right down **Lovat Lane**.

Picture the street in 1665. The walls of the houses would be where they are now, but the first and perhaps second floors cantilevered out to make more living space upstairs. This 'jettying' on both sides would result in only a metre's width for daylight to brighten the gloom. Horses were ridden along the middle of the street, and slops and 'night soil' thrown from upper windows accompanied by the traditional euphemistic warning of 'Gardez l'eau'. Wise pedestrians walked under the eaves of the first floor and consequently could hear the domestic disputes in the wooden houses. They became known as 'eavesdroppers'.

## Continue down Lovat Lane.

Enjoy the framed view of London's – and for the moment – Western Europe's tallest building, Renzo Piano's '**Shard**' at London Bridge.

## Turn left along Lower Thames Street.

Across the road is architect Horace Jones's **Billingsgate Fish Market**, closed in 1982 and refurbished by Richard Rogers as an exhibition space. The market has moved to the Isle of Dogs and the Corporation of London pay the borough of Tower Hamlets annual rent of 'one whole salmon' for the privilege.

## Turn left up St Mary at Hill.

Immediately on your left is the hall of the **Guild of Watermen and Lightermen**. The present Hall dates back to 1780 and remains the only original Georgian Hall in the City of London.

Watermen carry passengers and Lightermen carry freight. They undergo an arduous apprenticeship to master the dangerous quirks of the tidal River Thames. Thomas Doggett, an actor manager, backed his young boatman against all comers and in his will of 1715 established an annual race for graduating apprentices four miles (6.4km) upriver from Swan Lane Pier at London Bridge to the Swan pub in Chelsea. The winner has the honour of wearing the scarlet coat, breeches and silver arm badge that are based on the original costume of an 18th-century Waterman.

## Continue up the hill and take the first right into St Dunstan's Lane. This brings you to the ruined church of **St Dunstan**. Enter the churchyard to the left of the tower that houses the Wren complementary medicine

centre and bear right into the ruined nave.

The church was gutted on May 10th 1941 and as there was no parish for it to serve, never rebuilt. It is one of the hundred or so green spaces deliberately preserved within The City. If you want to hear the bells of St Dunstan's you still can. They ring out over a winery in the Napa Valley in California.

Up the hill, cross Great Tower Street, walk right and then left up Mark Lane. Turn right into Hart Street. On your right is **St Olave's Church.**

If the church is open to visitors you are welcome to go in. In the 1660s Samuel and Elizabeth Pepys worshipped and were both buried here.

But for one big thing, Samuel Pepys, as Secretary to the Navy, would be just a footnote in the history books. But he kept a diary – a secret diary in his own shorthand, involving backwards writing and foreign languages. It was not decoded until 1825. The diary reveals details of everyday life in intimate, scurrilous and amusing detail. Pepys was on personal terms with the King and had an eye, and more than that, for pretty young women. He was especially fond of actresses who had recently begun to appear on the English stage. His relationship with his wife Elizabeth was passionate and tempestuous. She held her ground, provocatively took lessons in the bedroom with a French dancing master and when Sam took an unhealthy interest in a new maid, threatened to emasculate him with red hot fire tongs.

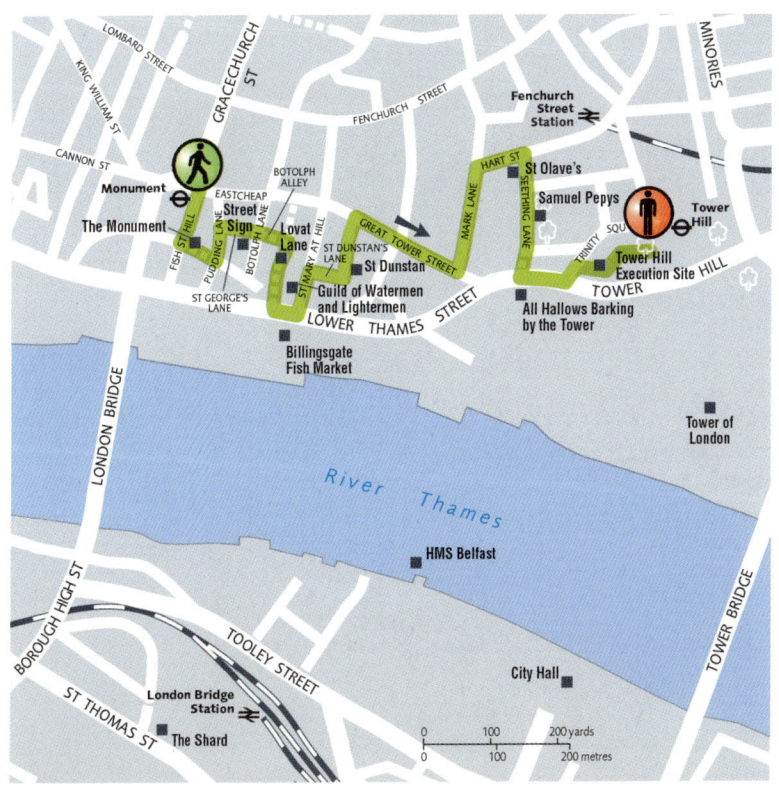

The Shard from the ruins of St Dunstan's Church

booties for geese to protect their feet.

This is one of the few City churches to survive the Great Fire of 1666, mainly thanks to Pepys and his friend William Penn – father of the founder of Pennsylvania – who pulled surrounding buildings down to create a fire break.

The hugger mugger claustrophobia of London helped the Great Fire to spread to such devastating effect, but in the previous year London had been visited by England's last major outbreak of bubonic plague. Up to a quarter of the 400,000 Londoners died. As soon as plague was diagnosed the entire family was locked in its house until they recovered or died.

Pepys wrote, 'I hear that a labourer I sent but the other day to Dagenham to know how they did there is dead of the plague and that one of my own watermen, that carried me daily, fell sick as soon as he had landed me on Friday morning last'.

Victims developed black soft swellings in their armpits and groins. These were the buboes or the plague tokens. The children's rhyme 'Ring a ring of roses' sounds innocent enough, but roses are the pattern of the buboes.

### Out of the church and right to Seething Lane.

Above the gate to the churchyard are the **skulls and crossbones** that inspired Charles Dickens to call it 'St Ghastly Grim'.

If the churchyard is open go in. Pepys had an entrance to his pew built in this side of the church, now bricked up, so that he could go direct from his office to church without getting wet. A "Mother Goose" was buried here in 1586. She reportedly was a nursemaid who sang rhymes and knitted little

Pocketful of posies' refers to the herbs and spices that people carried to sweeten the air. A-tishoo, we all fall down - symptoms of those close to death.

### Walk down Seething Lane with the garden on your left. Inside is a bust of Samuel Pepys.

'Seething' derives from the Old English for 'full of chaff or bran': the street was used for threshing corn for the market in Fenchurch Street.

Pepys' house was in the path of the fire and on the 3rd September he borrowed a cart "to carry away all my money, and plate, and best things". Carters charged 10 shillings/- (equivalent to £60) to move household goods. This rose to £40 (£3,000) by mid-week.

The following day he personally carried more items to a Thames barge, and later that evening "I did dig another hole, and put in my Parmazan cheese, as well as my wine and some other things."

### To the end of Seething Lane.

Across the road is the church of **All Hallows Barking by the Tower,** founded by nuns from Barking Abbey in 675 AD. The outside is part medieval, part Victorian and part reconstruction after severe bomb damage in World War II. The corporation had no plans to rebuild, but rector 'Tubby' Clayton, who'd founded the worldwide veterans' organisation Toc H in World War I, squatted here while contributions of materials came from Toc H members in Australia, Canada, USA, etc. The green spire is Zambian copper. In the crypt are the remains of a Roman pavement.

At the beginning of the Great Fire, Pepys and Penn watched it take hold from the tower, after which Pepys headed up river to inform the King.

### Go left then left again into Trinity Square and pass into the gardens.

Immediately inside the gate is the **Tower Hill execution site**.

Until 1747 this was the principal place of public execution for traitors who had been imprisoned in the Tower. The most notable of the 75 or so unfortunates who had their heads chopped off here are listed. From the Archbishop of Canterbury hacked to death in 1381 during the Peasants' Revolt, to Sir Thomas More and Charles II's illegitimate son, the Duke of Monmouth.

As a young boy, Pepys had witnessed the public execution of Charles I. Unlike most of his contemporaries he did not develop a taste for them, although he made a point of attending when a friend or acquaintance was scheduled to meet his end.

Trinity Square is associated with merchant shipping. Overlooked by the old Port of London Authority building, now a hotel, and by Trinity House, the lighthouse authority, you are surrounded by memorials to merchant sailors who lost their lives in the World Wars and the Falklands Conflict.

Enjoy a sandwich looking out towards the **Tower of London**. Beyond the Tower, the distinctive glass spherical **City Hall** -headquarters of the elected Greater London Authority. To its right, the Heavy Cruiser **HMS Belfast**, veteran of D-Day: built in 1939 she is now part of the Imperial War Museum.

Otherwise try 'The Liberty Bounds' or 'The Hung, Drawn and Quartered'.

## THAT MOST FRACTIOUS HAMLET IN THE TOWER DIVISION

# Spitalfields

**WALK 3**

In medieval England the fields here surrounded the hospital of St Mary. Used for recreation, by Londoners, from the 1680s Spitalfields attracted Huguenot silk weavers, in the 1880s Jewish refugees from Eastern Europe and, most recently, those from Bangladesh. Each brought its own take on the 'rag trade' and a new cuisine.

| Start | Finish | Distance | Refreshments |
|---|---|---|---|
| Liverpool Street Station | Liverpool Street Station | 1¼ miles (2.0km) | The Ten Bells |

Kindertransport Memorial

## ON THIS WALK

Kindertransport Memorial · Susannah Annesley · Dennis Severs · Dirty Dick's · Huguenot Weavers · The Water Poet

18 / WALK 3 – SPITALFIELDS

> From Liverpool St Station take the steps to the upper level and Liverpool Street itself.

On the concourse is a sculpted group of children, the **Kindertransport Memorial**. In November 1938, throughout Germany on 'Kristallnacht', Nazis smashed windows of Jewish shops and burnt down synagogues. The British Government agreed to waive immigration rules for unaccompanied children. Jewish groups and Quakers spirited away 10,000 to London via Hook of Holland, Harwich and then by train to Liverpool Street. All Germans between 16 and 70 were interned, but these children were fostered out to families: some sailed on to Canada. When boys reached 18 they were encouraged to join the forces: and many, young men and women with their fluent German were parachuted back behind enemy lines for 'Special Operations'.

> Go back into the station. Stay on the upper level and bear right towards Bishopsgate.

**Liverpool Street Station** occupies the site of the first Bethlehem Mental Hospital. This moved to Lambeth (now the Imperial War Museum) in the 1870s and this major terminal for East Anglia and Essex was built. See how far below you the platforms are. The original plan was to make a direct link with the recently extended Metropolitan Line. The best laid plans…

At the top of the escalators walk north keeping on the upper level (Great Eastern Walk) under the eaves of the Broadgate Centre offices.

In the 1890s Arthur Morrison called Spitalfields, 'that most fractious hamlet in the Tower Division'. Once notorious for free thinkers, religious non-conformists and squalor, Spitalfields maintains its quirky independence from the overbearing City. No Man's Land between the temples of Mammon and the true East End.

> Stop occasionally and glance across Bishopsgate.

The decorative Arts and Crafts **Bishopsgate Institute** has a vast reference library and specialises in adult education.

**Dirty Dick's** is a pub on the site of Nathaniel Bentley's house. In 1809, on the eve of their wedding, Bentley's fiancée died, so he left the wedding feast to decay in his dining room. He never washed again 'What's the point? If I wash, I only get dirty again!' Could this have given Dickens his inspiration for Miss Havisham?

There is a grand view past Peter Foggo's RBS building and beyond to Nicholas Hawksmoor's **Christ Church**.

> Cut left down the alley, Exchange Arcade, and into **Exchange Square** in the Broadgate Centre.

| Bud Flanagan | | Petticoat Lane | | Christ Church | |
|---|---|---|---|---|---|
| | Jack the Ripper | | London Jamme Masjid | | Spitalfields Market |

WALK 3 – SPITALFIELDS

*Huguenot weavers' houses off Brick lane*

The fine, bronze female figure is Fernando Botero's **'Broadgate Venus'**. Look beyond her where the flowing water feature mimics the River Walbrook that once flowed through The City and into the Thames. Picture the logistical nightmare beneath. Liverpool Street has 18 platforms, but the tracks are reduced to 6 immediately beyond the platforms.

### Walk to the right and under the building that seems to be hanging like a hammock above.

Foundations here must work round and between the railway lines. Much of this building's weight is supported by the arches above. At the top of the steps, look ahead at the **Broadgate Tower** (tall and thin) and **1 Bishopsgate** (short and fat). They are buttressed together like a medieval cathedral, weigh more or less the same and balance each other on a vast concrete platform.

### Turn right and cross Bishopsgate at the lights near Bruce Mclean's sculpture Eye-I, which gives a saucy wink to passers-by.

### Straight ahead into Spital Square and immediately right into Spital Yard.

Surrounded by modern offices, one much older house survives. **Susannah Annesley**, mother of John Wesley, was born here in 1669. See how the land level has risen in 350 years. Susannah was one of 25 children and she went on to have 19 herself. John, her fifteenth, became the founding father of Methodism. He despaired of the vast number of time-serving clerics in the Church of England and spent 50 years travelling the country in order to preach to anyone who'd listen. But John learnt much of what he preached from his formidable mother: when her husband was away on church business, Susannah grew so frustrated by the mealy mouthed efforts of his assistant that she took to holding open-air prayer meetings for her children and the parishioners. There was nothing mealy mouthed in her 'method' of bringing up children and much of John's message was originally hers: only faith and hard work will get you to heaven.

### Coming out of Spital Yard walk right.

**The Society for the Preservation of Ancient Building**s (SPAB) does what it says on the tin and is a fine example of a 1740s Huguenot house, although much restored. Next to it was the Central Foundation School for Girls of which only St Botolph's Hall, formerly their gym, remains. It is now rather a swish restaurant.

### Cross the road to the left and continue up Spital Square to Folgate Street. Turn left.

On your left, No. 18 has a weaver's bobbin hanging outside. This is **Dennis Severs**' house which dates from the 1720s. The Californian Severs made

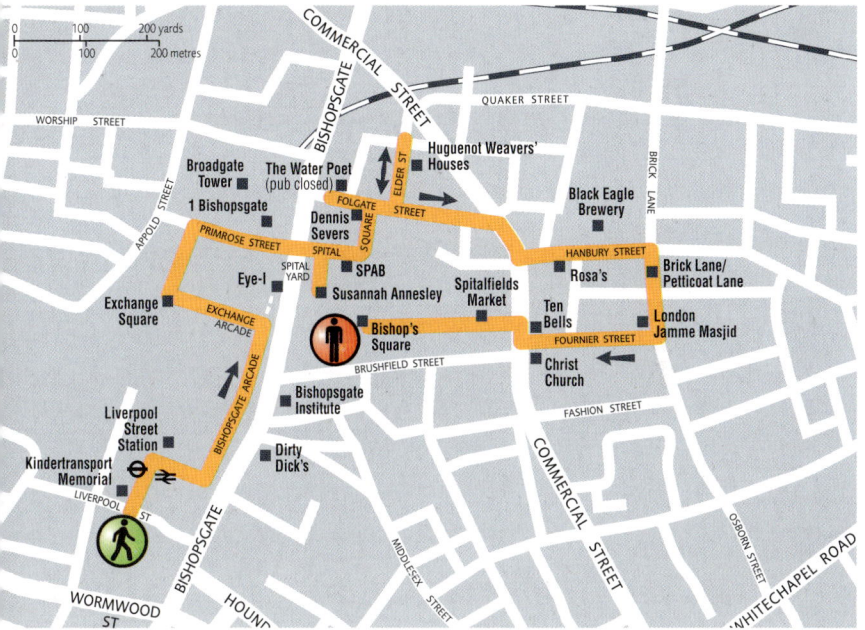

his home here in 1979. This area was dilapidated, but artists had started to move in. Severs arranged the ten rooms in different periods and called it "a still life drama". The opening times are on the shutters. Every day the curator fills the house with spontaneous details, flowers, food, casually discarded coats and freshly rumpled bed sheets – as if successive generations of the Jervis family that Severs invented, had just left a moment ago.

Opposite was the house of the Elizabethan poet John Taylor, by trade a waterman and called **The Water Poet** (after which the pub that stood here until 2019 took its name). He was the first writer to refer in print to Shakespeare's death. He also specialised in writing palindromes. 'Lewd I did live: evil did I dwel'. You can see how palindromes were easier to invent before spelling was standardised.

### Return along Folgate Street and go left into Elder Street.

These perfectly preserved **Huguenot weavers' houses** were on the verge of demolition in 1977 but Douglas Blain, a young Australian, led a campaign to save them by squatting in No. 7. With the support of other activists he formed the Spitalfields Trust. The poet John Betjeman invited the great and the good to an 'at home' in one of the squats 'Bailiffs Permitting'. Eventually Blain and his business partner Peter McKay raised enough money to buy, restore and sell on most of the street.

So, who were these Huguenot weavers? In 1685 the French King revoked the law that gave French Protestants the right to worship as they wished. Thousands fled the subsequent persecution and brought their weaving traditions to England. Silk weavers gravitated to Spitalfields and within half a century the local silk was recognised as among the finest in Europe. A century later, wars, new techniques, undercutting and taxes led to its decline and the area grew poorer and poorer. The houses have survived bombs and planners alike but each decade brings new threats of redevelopment.

### Back to Folgate Street and bear left. Cross Commercial Street safely, bearing right and then first left into Hanbury Street.

**Rosa's** was once a café owned by Francis Rossi's (Status Quo) auntie. Now it's rather a fine restaurant. Next door above Rosa's is a plaque. Reuben Weintraub was born here. He fought in the trenches of World War I. Weintraub so loathed his bullying sergeant that he vowed he'd make the man's name a laughing stock by using it as his stage name as a comedian. The sergeant was called Bud Flanagan: his name lives on, but not in the way Reuben hoped.

Eight years before Reuben saw the light of day on September 8th 1888, Annie Chapman's body was found outside this house. She was the second victim of the man/men/woman we know as 'Jack the Ripper'.

### Along Hanbury Street to Brick Lane.

On the left stands Ben Truman's **Black Eagle Brewery**. By 1873 it was the largest brewery in the world. Much of it has been preserved and converted to artists' workshops, alternative shopping outlets, cafés and street food.

### At Brick Lane turn right.

### Or if you fancy a slight diversion, go left and indulge yourself in the Middle Eastern hookah joints or one of the legendary Jewish bagel and salt beef cafés. Otherwise, head right, down Brick Lane into Banglatown.

At the end of the 19th century Ashkenazi Jews in flight from the pogroms of East Europe settled here. The tradition of first class tailoring added a new textile dimension to East London's 'rag trade'. The market is in **Petticoat Lane** at the far end of Brick Lane, though it hasn't officially been called this since the 1820s - too rude. Nowadays most Jewish businesses have moved on and the area is dominated by immigrants from Bangladesh, who thankfully continue the traditions of selling fine textiles and good food.

No matter what time of day, you will be encouraged – at a special discount – to eat at one of the many curry houses. Whether you resist the temptation or not, make your way to the minaret on the corner of Fournier Street.

The **London Jamme Masjid** (Great Mosque) is the only building outside Jerusalem to have served each of the three Abrahamic religions. Built in 1743 as a Huguenot chapel, it became a Methodist church, then in 1897 a synagogue and from 1975 has been a mosque.

### Walk right along Fournier Street.

One of the grandest of Huguenot streets, it's been popular with young British artists since the 1970s. Tracey Emin lived here: Gilbert and George still do. Some windows have shutters on the outside in the French style and others inside, better suited to colder climates like Holland and Britain.

### Back at Commercial Street.

On your right is the **Ten Bells** pub where Annie Chapman and Jack the Ripper's fifth and final victim, Mary Kelly, were last seen.

The Ripper is the most notorious denizen of these streets. Whatever you read or hear nobody, but nobody, knows for sure who perpetrated the five murders. There is a mighty industry built around that autumn of 1888 and plenty of opportunity to hear the gruesome details on a special 'Ripper Tour', but for now...

On your left is the monumental **Christ Church**. The Fifty Churches Act of 1710 was intended to provide fifty new churches for the expanding population of London. Twelve were eventually built, including all those of Nicholas Hawksmoor. If it's open, go in. The church, like much in Spitalfields, has been lovingly restored.

## Cross the road and into Spitalfields Market.

Christ Church

Licensed in 1682 by King Charles II for the sale of 'Flesh, Fowl and Roots' it became a fruit and veg market under Robert Horner in 1876. In 1991, the official market moved out to Leyton and since then it has at times struggled to find a new identity. But gradually one emerged: organic food, ethnic clothes, a relaxed counter culture ethos, especially on Sunday when the market stalls are fully stretched.

## Walk through the market on the left-hand side.

When the novelist Jeanette Winterson had a house here some years back she was offered £60,000 per annum by Starbuck's to open a coffee house on the ground floor. To her credit, she refused and opened her own shop (40 Brushfield Street, since closed). Nowadays, if you're desperate for a Starbuck's, you won't have to look far.

## You are now in Bishop's Square

recently developed by Norman Foster: preservation groups who opposed the development failed to stop it. Pubs – try The Gun or Ten Bells, or there are countless cafés and restaurants in the market and beyond.

## TO THE BANKS OF THE FLEET

# Smithfield

Smithfield has been London's meat market for a thousand years. The blood of sheep, cows, pigs, poultry and people flowed here. No longer a live trading market nor thankfully an execution site, we can turn our minds to London's oldest hospital and the peaceful monks of the Charterhouse for solace.

| Start | Finish | Distance | Refreshments |
|---|---|---|---|
| St Paul's | Farringdon | 1 mile (1.6km) | The Castle |

*Entrance to St Bartholomew the Great*

## ON THIS WALK

- Postman's Park
- St Bartholomew's Hospital
- Medieval execution site
- St Bartholomew the Great
- Cloth Fair
- Barbican

**Leave St Paul's station by exit 1 on the corner of Cheapside and St Martin's le Grand.**

**Cheapside** was the main shopping street and ceremonial route of the medieval city. 'Cheap' being Old English for 'market'. On the south side is the church of **St Mary le Bow**, its steeple topped with a copper dragon 3 metres long. It has a ring of 12 bells and anyone born within the sound of Bow Bells can be considered a true cockney.

**Walk north up St Martin's le Grand.**

Just past the **Lord Raglan** pub is a plaque to show where Aldersgate once stood. One of the seven gates of medieval London that were closed each night when Bow Bells sounded the curfew.

**Cross at the controlled crossing and go into St Botolph's churchyard, now known as Postman's Park. If the gates are locked then take Little Britain heading west.**

Botolph was a 7th-century Abbot who became the patron saint of travellers. There was a church dedicated to him outside each city gate. Before leaving the relative security of the city a medieval traveller would confess and make a gift to the church. On safe arrival at Norwich, Lincoln or York he would immediately visit a St Botolph's there and give thanks for his safe passage. The Abbot's home town in Lincolnshire became Botolphstown, later shortened to Boston.

On the far side of Postman's Park under a sheltered area is a wall, part covered with hand-lettered Doulton tiles. They commemorate young and old who lost their lives trying to save others. This was the brainchild of G F Watts who regretted the fact that only the upper classes were considered worthy of official recognition, so he established this public memorial to commemorate 'Heroic Self Sacrifice' by ordinary people who might otherwise have been forgotten.

**Leave Postman's Park through the opposite gate.**

To the left, the statue is that of **Rowland Hill** who in 1840 introduced the postage stamp. Previously the recipient paid on receipt of a letter. When Hill was 8 years old he was sent to the pawn shop so that his mother could afford to open a letter. He grew up believing that if more people were able to send letters, then more people would learn to read and write. A penny black postage stamp would guarantee the letter's arrival anywhere in the country the very next day.

Behind him, the former Central London Post Office is now part of Merrill Lynch/Bank of America.

**Turn right, cross at the controlled crossing and walk straight down Little Britain. Stop**

WALK 4 – SMITHFIELD

when you get to Smithfield.

Little Britain is thought to be named after Robert le Bretoun who inherited several houses here in 1274.

All around you is **St Bartholomew's Hospital**, known since its foundation by Rahere in 1123 as plain 'Bart's'.

Rahere was a courtier, perhaps jester to King Henry I, second son of William the Conqueror. In 1120 the court was plunged into gloom when the king's eldest son was drowned at sea. Rahere 'gave up the idle pursuits of his youth' and made a pilgrimage to Rome where he contracted Roman Fever – a form of malaria. He was nursed back to health in a monastery reputed to contain the relics of Saint Bartholomew. Rahere vowed that, if he recovered, he would build a hospital for the poor in London. On his way home, Saint Bartholomew appeared in his dreams and commanded him to build a church to the glory of God in a suburb of London called Smoothfield. Rahere became both Prior of St Bartholomew the Great and master of the hospital.

Over the years its clinicians have included doctors Harvey (circulation of the blood), Parkinson (Parkinson's Disease), Langdon-Down (Down's Syndrome) and Barnardo (child welfare). It also witnessed the first meeting of Sherlock Holmes and Doctor Watson. 'How are you?' he said cordially, 'You have been in Afghanistan, I perceive.'

In the 1990s the future of Bart's was called into question but remains open as a specialist cancer and cardiac hospital, whilst general hospital services are concentrated at the Royal London in Whitechapel.

## Look around you in **Smithfield**.

Straight ahead is London's main wholesale meat market, but first recall that this open space was at times a tournament field for knights, and above all London's place of public execution for 400 years. In 1600, that grisly activity moved to Tyburn – or Marble Arch as we now know it.

Here in 1305 William Wallace, who fought for Scottish freedom, was hanged, drawn and quartered. To the left there is a memorial. He has the distinction of being the first 'traitor' to have his head impaled on a spike on London Bridge.

Wat Tyler led the rebels of the Peasants' Revolt here to meet the 14 year old King Richard II in 1381. While making their grievances clear, Tyler upset the Lord Mayor of London who stabbed him. He was rushed into Bart's, but the wound was fatal. With great sang-froid, the young king took control of the situation, the ringleaders were rounded up and the rest drifted back home.

In the 1500s, Henry VIII had a cook boiled alive for poisoning his master: his daughter Mary burned over 200 Protestant Martyrs; her sister Elizabeth behaved in a similar fashion towards Roman Catholics. All while England sorted out whether to be Protestant or Catholic.

For light relief, look at the gateway to the churchyard of **St Bartholomew the Great** on your right. It was covered in plaster until 1917 when a zeppelin dropped a bomb in Smithfield. The blast cracked the plaster and revealed the half timbering we see today.

## Walk through the arch and into the churchyard.

Before Henry VIII demolished half the church you would have been walking inside the nave. All that remains is the Quire. Don't be fooled by the flinty Victorian exterior. Inside is a precious, unspoilt example of 12th-century Norman architecture. If it's your only chance to visit, do go in. It will cost a few pounds: they have started charging because it is expensive to maintain and so popular because many films have used it as a location. 'Four Weddings and a Funeral', 'Shakespeare in Love', 'Amazing Grace', 'Elizabeth', 'The Other Boleyn Girl', etc.

Among the treasures inside are Rahere's tomb and a delightful epitaph by John Whiting for his parents from 1681:
*'She first deceased, he for little tried, To live without her, liked it not and died.'*

**Go through the gate at the other end of the churchyard into Cloth Fair. Walk to your right.**

As you do this, glance back to your left to see a blue plaque to the poet **John Betjeman** who was born and lived in Clerkenwell. He was a prime mover in preserving the Victorian heritage of London, including St Pancras station where his jolly statue stands cheering up weary Eurostar travellers.

In 1133 Rahere established an annual cloth fair in Smithfield. He was able to charge tolls and so raised funds for his Priory. It began on the eve of St Bartholomew's Day, 24th August, lasted 3 days and became known as Bartholomew Fair. Even though he was Prior, Rahere was not above performing juggling tricks at the fair.

**Halfway down Cloth Fair on the right is the Hand and Shears pub.**

Any trader found guilty of cheating would be brought to judgement at the Hand and Shears.

A temporary court was held in the pub, called the Court of Piepowder, wherein justice might be done while the boots of the parties were yet white with the dust of the highway – from the French 'Cour de Pie-poudre'. The cases

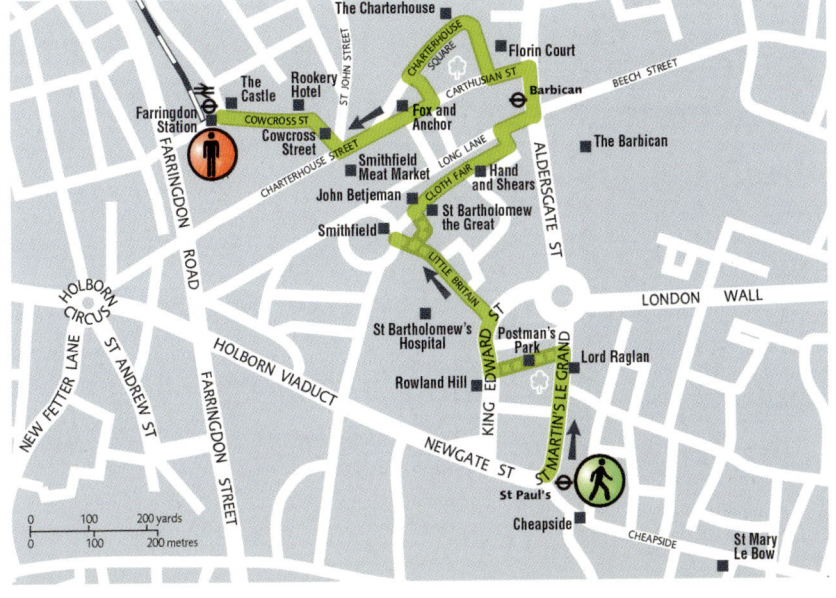

which came before it were mainly for trading without licences, not having the freedom of the city or for selling with false measures.

For years puritans tried to get the fair banned, but only in 1855 were the City authorities able to suppress it on the grounds that it encouraged, drunkenness, crime and debauchery.

## Join Long Lane to the junction with Aldersgate Street.

Gaze in wonder at the towers, Shakespeare, Cromwell and Lauderdale, and the 2,400 apartments of the Barbican Centre. **The Barbican** is named after the fortified watchtower built to keep watch over the approaches to Aldersgate in the 13th century. This area, devastated by incendiary bombs on December 29th 1940, remained undeveloped for years. The Corporation of London became concerned that so few people were now living within the Square Mile and they commissioned architects, Chamberlin, Powell and Bon, to design these apartments. They did so in the fashionable style of the time – neo-brutalism. The complex now houses most of the people who live in The City, as well as a concert hall, cinemas and theatre.

## Go left up Aldersgate past Barbican station entrance and take the first left down Carthusian Street. Turn right at the gates of Charterhouse Square.

**Florin Court** on your right, a distinctive 1930s block of 'businessmen's' flats, is recognisable as the home of Hercule Poirot in the TV series. The garden around which you are walking is a 'key' garden for residents only. It covers a plague pit dating from the Black Death of 1348/9, which devastated Western Europe.

## Continue half way round the square - under the gas lights - to the arched entrance to **The Charterhouse**.

Walter de Manny established the Charterhouse where monks could pray for the souls of the plague dead. Carthusian is a strict order in which monks spend most of their lives alone in prayer and penance. In 1535, Prior John Houghton refused to sign up to The Act of Supremacy which made Henry VIII head of the Church of England. He was hanged, drawn and quartered and his arm nailed to the door of The Charterhouse 'pour encourager les autres'. Six of his monks were executed and ten taken to Newgate Prison where they died of gaol fever.

After the Dissolution, Charterhouse passed through many hands until in 1603 Thomas Sutton, the wealthiest commoner in the land, established Charterhouse School and an alms house for elderly, but worthy, men. In the 19th century the school moved to Godalming in Surrey, but this is still a home for 40 gentlemen pensioners.

## Continue past the Malmaison Hotel and through the gates into Charterhouse Street.

To your right is the **Fox and Anchor Inn**, one of the few examples of Art Nouveau in London. The working day in the meat market ends by 6 in the morning and when licensing laws were stricter a special case was made. This is one of the local pubs famous for its Smithfield Breakfast. On the menu - sweet cured bacon, pork and leek sausage, eggs (any style), grilled tomato, white and black pudding, hash browns, minute steak, lambs' kidneys, baked beans, fried bread, chicken liver and mushrooms. And of course, a pint of stout.

## Cross St John Street and into Cowcross Street.

Before going down **Cowcross Street**, look left at Horace Jones' Smithfield Meat Market. Ornamental dragons and shields proclaim that this is still very much part of the City of London.

No need to think too hard about how the street got its name, harder to imagine the herds and flocks being driven down it. Smithfield was a live market until 1855 when drovers delivered cattle, sheep, geese and turkeys from all corners of England. Sometimes, in cahoots with thieves, they were known to stampede cattle causing chaos which would enable them to loot the shops. It's believed to be where the phrase 'Bull in a China Shop' comes from, although most of the shops here were related to the use of every part of the animals slaughtered in the market – leather tanners, glue making, horners, feather beds…

Charles Dickens had Oliver Twist and Bill Sykes pass through here in the 1830s:
'The ground was covered, nearly ankle-deep, with filth and mire; a thick steam rising from the reeking bodies of the cattle. Countrymen, butchers, drovers, hawkers, boys, thieves, idlers, and vagabonds of every low grade, were mingled together in a mass; the whistling of drovers, the barking dogs, the bellowing and plunging of the oxen, the bleating of sheep, the grunting and squeaking of pigs, the cries of hawkers, the shouts, oaths, and quarrelling on all sides…'

## Go along Cowcross Street, past the Rookery Hotel on the right.

The upmarket **Rookery Hotel** is ironically named. When luxury goods were taxed during the Napoleonic Wars, this prosperous area went into steep decline and the slum tenements that covered Clerkenwell by the middle of the 19th century were known as Rookeries. Police no-go areas but wonderful material for the young Charles Dickens.

## Stop at **Farringdon Station**.

How thrilled a child would have been to ride on the world's first underground line from Paddington to Farringdon in 1863. It changed the nature of the area and introduced the idea of commuting. New ways brushed against old in 1868 when families could travel by underground railway with their picnic baskets to watch London's last public hanging outside Newgate Prison.

## Look to **The Castle** pub.

The present pub was built in the late 1800s. You will see that it has three golden balls, the sign of a pawnbroker, outside. This is to commemorate the night when the then Prince of Wales, later George IV, ran out of money while gambling nearby. He sent his man to borrow money, leaving a watch as surety. He redeemed the watch next day and The Castle is now the only pub to double as a registered pawnbroker.

Try The Castle or there are many well-known chain cafés and a couple of family-run Italian restaurants.

This walk leads straight into the next one.

# MONKS, NUNS AND THE DISPOSSESSED

# Clerkenwell

**WALK 5**

Clerkenwell, just outside The City, has had a roller coaster history. From monastic pastoral to the arrival of wealthy Huguenot weavers who made it prosperous; a hundred years later among the most pitiable slums in London; now a fashionable enclave of architects' practices and bijou loft conversions. And indeed one of the most unexpected Grade I-listed buildings in London.

**Start:** Farringdon
**Finish:** The Angel
**Distance:** ¾ mile (1.4km)
**Refreshments:** In Exmouth Market

Frieze of gin manufacture, Britton Street

## ON THIS WALK

- St John's Garden
- St John's Gate
- Thomas Britton
- Booth's Gin Distillery
- Docwra Memorial Garden
- Clerkenwell Green

30 / WALK 5 – CLERKENWELL

London Underground, Thameslink and the new Elizabeth Line make Farringdon Station a major railway hub. **From the station go left up Faulkner's Alley off Cowcross Street, next to the Castle pub,** to remind you that in the first half of the 19th century Clerkenwell had perhaps the highest murder rate and concentration of criminality in London. **Come out into Benjamin Street and turn right.**

**If the passage is closed, go north up Turnmill Street. Turnmill Street** may well take its name from a medieval watermill on the River Fleet that once flowed along the route of the present Metropolitan Line. **After 30 metres, turn right into Benjamin Street.**

Either way, cut through **St John's Garden** to your left, to try out the idiosyncratic park benches designed by art students in a competition sponsored by Bloomberg in the 1990s. At the end of the park directly opposite on the corner of Britton Street is a **distinctive house** with blue Belgian glazed pantiles, variations of brick colour, flamboyant trellis work and diamond shaped windows. It was commissioned from Piers Gough of CZWG Architects in 1987 by journalist and former President of the Ramblers' Association Janet Street Porter. She lived here for 15 years.

**Now go left up Britton Street.**

The street was laid out in 1718 and the first few houses on your left are among the best preserved in the area. Some shutters are inside the windows in the local style and others outside in the French. The top floors would have been the workshops of weavers or clockmakers, below them the family rooms and at ground level perhaps a shop.

**Continue to the corner of Briset Street.**

Look up at the imposing façade on your left. F W Pomeroy carved this **frieze of gin manufacture**. The wall from the 1778 Booth's Gin Distillery used to be the other side overlooking Turnmill Street, but it was preserved and moved. The pure, plentiful water from the springs of Clerkenwell was ideal for gin. The drink was introduced from the Netherlands in 1688 by the court of the new Dutch King William III. The early years of the next century saw such plentiful harvests and the low price of corn led to cheap gin. By the mid-18th century there were 6,000 dram shops in London. Per capita consumption by the 1730s was 2 pints a week, including children.

In 1751, Henry Fielding the novelist said, 'Should the drinking of this poison be continued at this present height during the next 20 years there will by that time be very few of the common people left to drink it.' Duties were imposed by Parliament to curb its consumption and increase the exchequer. From the 18th to the early 20th centuries the streets of Clerkenwell thronged with barrels and

| Karl Marx | | Clerks' Well | | Finsbury Health Centre | |
|---|---|---|---|---|---|
| | Red Fleet | | Peabody Buildings | | Joe Grimaldi |

WALK 5 – CLERKENWELL

horses and carts.

Apart from Booth's there were a number of other distilleries established here by the mid-18th century - Stones, Tanqueray, Gordon's and Nicholson's.

### Down Briset St to St John's Lane. On your left is **St John's Gate**.

This gate was built by Prior Thomas Docwra in 1504. The Priory had been founded in 1140 by the Anglo-Norman knight Jordan de Briset for the Knights Hospitaller of St John. They cared for the sick and poor, specifically, Crusaders and Pilgrims to the Holy Land. The Order was repressed in England during the Reformation but continued abroad.

Attempts to re-establish its work by a group of committed followers in 19th-century Britain did not meet with the approval of the Grand Master in Malta, so they started their own St John Ambulance Association to train ordinary people in First Aid. The Brigade was formed in 1887 with ambulance facilities and a commitment to provide First Aid to the public. They took the white Maltese cross as their emblem.

Queen Victoria was so impressed by their voluntary work, that she established an order of chivalry, the Most Venerable Order of St John, to recognise significant voluntary service to the community.

### Walk under the Gate.

If the **Museum** at the Gate is open, do go in. It's free and interesting. If you're lucky your visit might coincide with one of the free guided tours. Collections of the Order are on display, illustrating the history and work of the Knights Hospitaller from the time of the Crusades to the present day.

Do, as you go through the gate, feel for the hinge on the left-hand side. It is the original top hinge of the wooden gate itself. So low because in 500 years land levels have risen substantially. We build on the past. Through the gate an old blocked up doorway to your right as you emerge confirms this.

**St John's Square** was the open space around which the cloisters were constructed. Here would have been the stables, hospital, all the necessary activities to sustain the brothers – kitchens, bakery, brewery. Now busy Clerkenwell Road cuts through it.

### Into the Square and carefully cross Clerkenwell Road.

To your right is the **Docwra Memorial Garden** to St John Ambulance personnel who died in World War II. The red-brick building beyond it is the

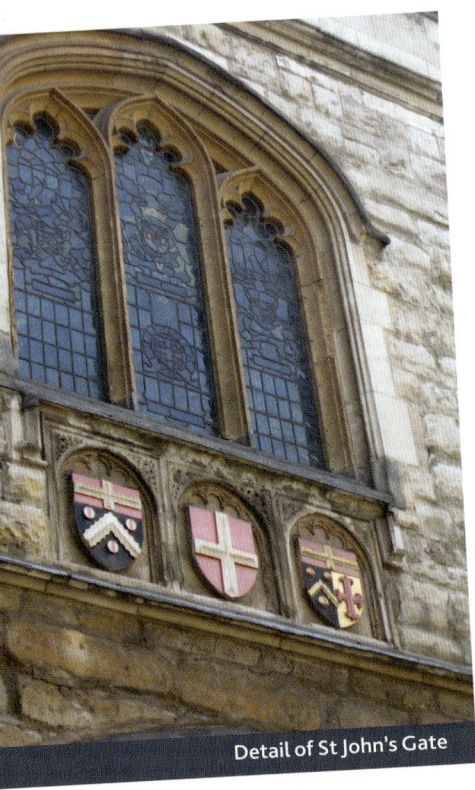

Detail of St John's Gate

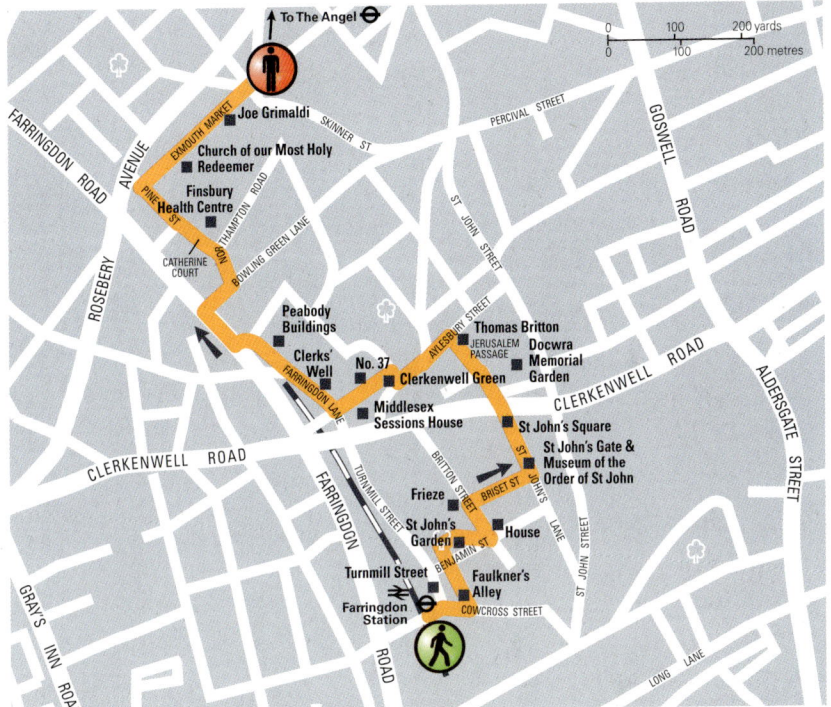

church. The dark stone semicircle on the pavement describes the perimeter of the original church burnt down during the Peasants' Revolt of 1381. A new gothic church was then built and this survived until destroyed by bombs in May 1941.

If it is open, go in and visit the surviving 12th-century crypt beneath.

## Go along Jerusalem Passage, passing The Dovetail (Belgian Bar).

High at the end of the passage on the right is a green plaque to **Thomas Britton**, a self-taught small-coal (charcoal) merchant in Clerkenwell. In 1678, he established a weekly concert series in what was a tumbledown former stable. He opened his upper room, and the likes of George Frederick Handel and Johann Pepusch would clamber up the rickety outside wooden staircase. The concert series ran for thirty-six years.

## Turn left and into **Clerkenwell Green**.

Yes, it was once green: a public area between The Priory of St John and Nunnery of St Mary to the north. There were cloisters where The Crown public house is now. By the time Dickens wrote 'Oliver Twist', he said "it was called, by some perversion of terms, 'The Green'." A centre of the radical book trade, it was here that Mr Brownlow, while browsing, no doubt at an 'anti-establishment' book stall, had his handkerchief swiped by the Artful Dodger.

The Green has for two centuries been associated with radical causes.

In 1826, William Cobbett addressed thousands against The Corn Laws. Loaves of bread draped in black and purple were paraded round the Green

Middlesex Sessions House

in mock funerals, carried on hearses. In 1838, the Tolpuddle Martyrs were welcomed back to England after their transportation sentence had ended. In 1870, Eleanor Marx (daughter of Karl) campaigned here for Votes for Women. Tiny Eleanor had to go into The Crown to borrow a beer crate to stand on because so many turned up. Ever since, May Day and anti-war rallies have congregated here for the march to Trafalgar Square.

**Walk down the right-hand side to the white building with the red door, 37 Clerkenwell Green.**

Built in 1727 as a Welsh Charity School, it became a shop, a pub and by the mid-19th century Karl Marx held meetings here. By 1900 it had become a left wing press supported by William Morris and G B Shaw. Local resident, Vladimir Lenin, printed his pamphlet Iskra (The Spark), on tissue type paper to smuggle into Tsarist Russia.

The imposing 18th-century building over the road to the left is the **Middlesex Sessions House**. This local courthouse, now used by Ennismore Events, could sentence criminals to transportation. If guilty they were whisked through the back of the court straight onto a boat down the River Fleet to the hulks at Blackfriars. Now it is being developed as a mixed use business, retail and leisure complex.

**Keep the courthouse on your left and turn right; walk up Farringdon Lane which traces the old bank of the River Fleet.**

In Roman times, drinkable and navigable, the Fleet shrank and grew so polluted through the years it became known as the 'Red Fleet'. In the early 1700s, Jonathan Swift wrote in 'A Description of a City Shower':-
'Sweepings from Butchers' stalls, dung, guts and blood,
Drowned puppies, stinking sprats, all drenched in mud,
Dead cats and turnip tops come tumbling down the flood.'

**On your right, behind a closed door, is the original Clerks' Well.**

Pure spring water gushed from the walls of the long-destroyed nunnery, where each Easter the Worshipful Company of Parish Clerks would perform dramatized scenes from the Bible in their Miracle or Mystery Plays.

**Continue up the hill past the Betsey Trotwood pub.**

The **Peabody Buildings** on your right are just one of the many blocks of flats created in the 19th century by the great American philanthropist George Peabody for low paid workers. Peabody was buried with great fanfare in Westminster Abbey. Then they read his will and discovered he wished to be laid to rest in his native Massachusetts. So, his body was disinterred and carried across the Atlantic on HMS *Monarch*.

**Turn right into Bowling Green Lane, immediately left up Northampton Road and left again into Catherine Court.**

On your right is the **Finsbury Health Centre**. Perhaps a little dilapidated and in need of refurbishment, this is up there with St Paul's and Westminster Abbey as a Grade I-listed building. Created by Berthold Lubetkin in the 1930s as part of the Finsbury Plan – a prototype National Health Service. Tuberculosis, rickets and many other diseases associated with deprivation were endemic, so a TB clinic, foot clinic, dental surgery, and solarium were incorporated. The basement had facilities for cleaning and disinfecting bedclothes, and a lecture theatre and mortuary were also included. Lubetkin wanted people to feel welcome but never patronised. He also wanted the Centre to be like a club, or a drop-in centre.

**Carry on ahead along Pine Street and turn right into Exmouth Market.**

Stave off your hunger pangs for a few minutes and visit the **Church of our Most Holy Redeemer**. It looks like a Roman Catholic church in many ways but is High Anglican. Farther down the market on the right is a plaque to London's first great clown, **Joe Grimaldi**. Son of an Italian immigrant, he became the most popular entertainer in town with his virtuoso athletic clowning. So athletic that he was riddled with arthritis by 40, but left a heritage of face painting and the name, Joey the Clown.

In Exmouth Market you'll find as many cafés and restaurants and food stalls as anyone might need. If you wish, head up Rosebery Avenue to the Junction Angel, where you'll find many more and an underground station to boot.

WALK 5 – CLERKENWELL / 35

# THE LIBERTY OF THE BISHOP OF WINCHESTER

# The South Bank

In Tudor times the City of London frowned on theatre, prostitution and bear baiting: Southwark, on the south bank, did not. As London Bridge closed for the night, watermen did a roaring trade carrying passengers across the river: but if the Thames froze, you could walk onto the ice and entertainment was brought to you!

| Start | Finish | Distance | Refreshments |
|---|---|---|---|
| Embankment | London Bridge | 2 miles (3.2km) | The George Inn |

St Paul's Cathedral from the South Bank

## ON THIS WALK

- Royal Festival Hall
- OXO Tower
- Tate Modern
- South Bank Arts Centre
- Gabriel's Wharf
- Millennium Bridge

**Leave Embankment station on the river side, turn immediately right on to Hungerford Bridge. Cross the river.**

Ahead is the site of the Festival of Britain (1951) when the government tried to cheer the nation up after the dangers and privations of war. The **Royal Festival Hall** is the sole survivor and is now the centrepiece of the South Bank Arts Centre. The riverside is well stocked with restaurants and cafés after its refurbishment in 2007.

**Turn left along 'The Queen's Walk'.**

On the other side of the river is **Cleopatra's Needle**, at 3,500 years the oldest landmark in London. Sent as a present from the Turkish Viceroy of Egypt, as thanks for defeating Napoleon, it eventually arrived in 1877. Two sphinxes were cast in bronze and the Metropolitan Board of Works erected them the wrong way round. They should be on guard facing away from the obelisk.

In the 1970s other elements of the **South Bank Arts Centre** were added in the fashionable neo-brutalist style. As you approach Waterloo Bridge the cavernous area beneath the Queen Elizabeth Hall is home to skateboarders and graffiti artists under constant threat of eviction. Beneath the bridge is the British Film Institute with bookstalls outside, and just beyond that the **National Theatre**. For a hundred years theatre people had dreamt of a permanent national theatre and eventually, after residency at the Old Vic under the direction of Laurence Olivier, the new theatre opened in 1976. Olivier lived long enough to see his dream become reality and one of the three theatres in this complex is named after him.

**Pass the statue of Olivier as Henry V.**

Look across the river again at the ships moored on the north bank. They cater for parties and conferences, but the white ship in the middle has another function. **HQS Wellington** is the Company Hall of the Worshipful Company of Master Mariners, the only London Livery Company to have its hall outside the old City walls. To its right, see the Middle and Inner Temples with their chapels and gardens. These are two of the Inns of Court where law students are trained in advocacy and emerge as barristers.

Look ahead at the **OXO Tower**. In the 1920s, the manufacturers of the beef stock OXO cube planned a tower with illuminated signs advertising their product. When the City of London refused permission for this blatant advertising, the tower was built with four sets of windows, each of which "coincidentally" happened to be in the shapes of a circle, a cross and a circle.

**Gabriel's Wharf** on your right is the brainchild of the Coin Street

| Cardinal Cap Alley | The Clink Gaol | Southwark Cathedral |
| Globe Theatre | Golden Hind | Borough Market |

WALK 6 – THE SOUTH BANK

Community Builders. Just over forty years ago the South Bank was bleak, unattractive, had few shops and a weak local economy. Local residents mounted an extraordinary campaign to buy 13 acres (5.25 hectares) of derelict land, since developed into a thriving neighbourhood with design shops, galleries, restaurants, cafés and bars.

The small park next door is **Bernie Spain Gardens**, named after Bernadette Spain, a local campaigner on health and housing provisions for the area's residents in the 1980s.

### Walk under the OXO Tower and Blackfriars Bridge along The Jubilee Walkway.

In medieval times Dominican Friars had a large monastery on the north bank. Although it was demolished by Henry VIII in 1538, Londoners have long memories. When the first bridge was built here in the 1760s, the government called it William Pitt Bridge after the former Prime Minister. But no, the locals thought different and insisted on calling it Blackfriars.

**Blackfriars** is the only London railway station to span the River Thames.

You are approaching the former Bankside Power Station, refurbished as **Tate Modern**, which houses London's major collection of modern art. Entry is free and even if you don't have time to study more than a few exhibits, take the lift to the café at the top. There you can treat yourself to a view of the thrilling skyline of the City of London, still dominated by Christopher Wren's masterpiece, **St Paul's Cathedral**. This took 35 years to build (1679-1714) and is the only cathedral in the world to be completed within its architect's lifetime. Almost the first and last example of the English Baroque style which had

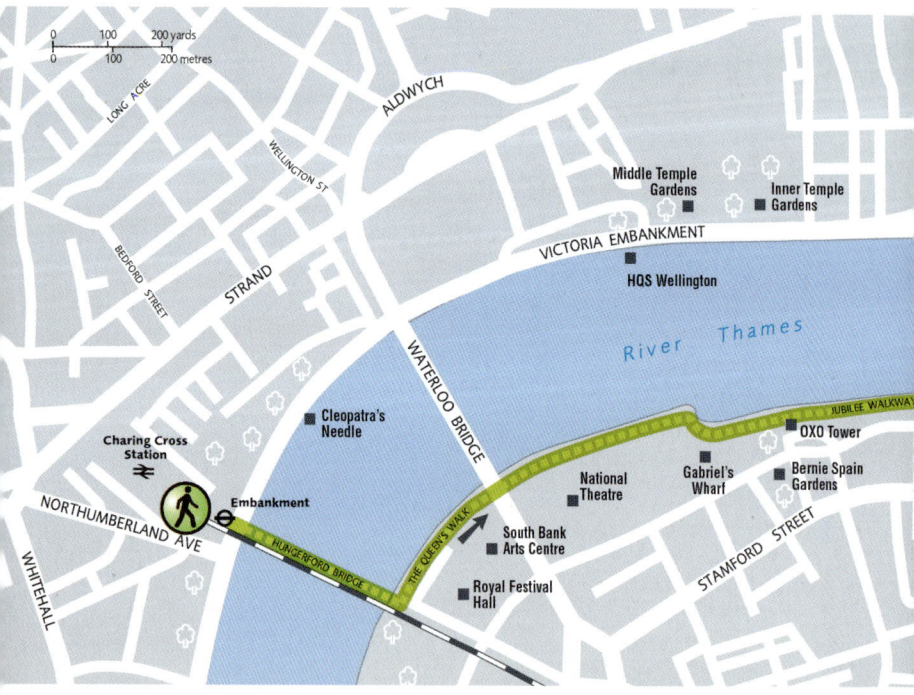

become unfashionable by the time it was completed.

The **Millennium Bridge** was opened in the year 2000 to link these two impressive buildings, but things don't always work out as they're planned. As people walked across, the bridge swayed from side to side and had to be closed. The problem was apparently 'synchronous lateral excitation' caused by the rhythmic tramping of feet. Stabilisers were fitted, the bridge was re-opened two years later, but it had lost its status as The Millennium Bridge and will forever be known as 'The Wobbly Bridge'.

A brick-built terrace, Nos. 50-52 Bankside is home to the Provost of Southwark Cathedral and adjoins **Cardinal Cap Alley**. No. 49 Bankside, the three-storey house to its left is an early 18th-century building with a bell pull that sounds on the roof garden. Some believe, wrongly, that this is where Wren stayed while building St Paul's. It was only built in 1710, by which time Wren was in his eighties and only the finishing touches had to be made on his cathedral.

What cannot be airbrushed from history is that Cardinal Cap Alley led down to a brothel called the Cardinal's Hat. Yes, these were the **Stews of Southwark**.

In medieval times and beyond, the City of London wouldn't license prostitution: Southwark, under the jurisdiction of the Bishop of Winchester, did. When London Bridge closed at curfew and the day's work was done, Watermen transported those seeking such diversions across the river. On the south bank, wearing long white gloves the 'Winchester Geese' waved potential trade ashore. For more wholesome entertainment there were four theatres but of course they could only perform in daylight.

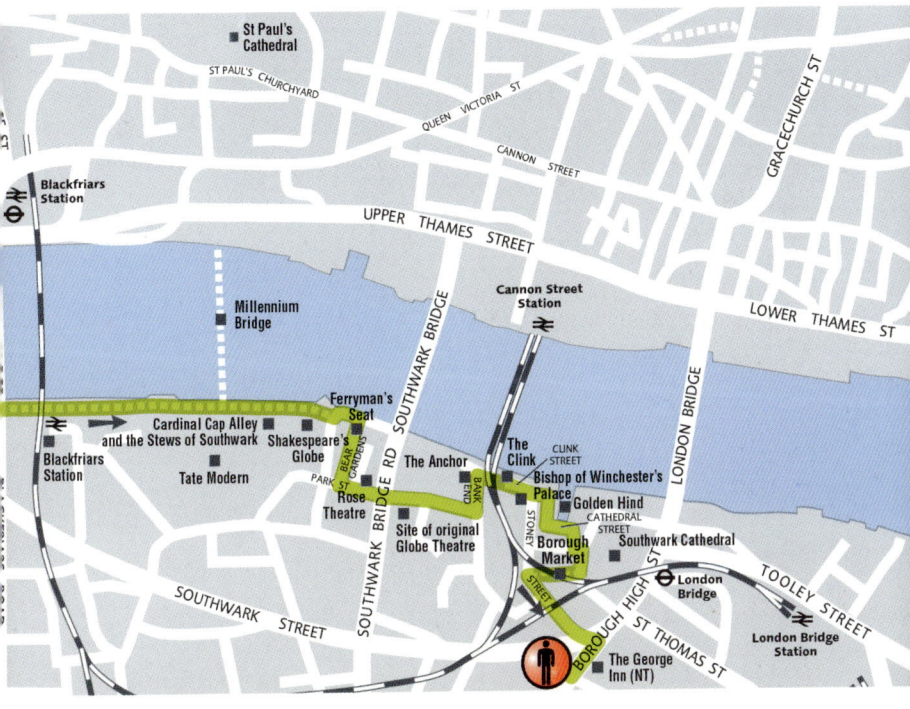

WALK 6 – THE SOUTH BANK / 39

Two rival companies dominated Elizabethan theatre: the Lord Admiral's Men at the Rose, and the Lord Chamberlain's Men at The Globe. Our most influential playwright William Shakespeare worked mostly for the latter.

**Shakespeare's Globe** was created in the 1990s using building methods and materials to make it an exact replica of the 16th-century original. When American actor Sam Wanamaker came to England in 1949 he was astonished that no trace or memorial remained to commemorate Elizabethan Theatre. He made it his life's work to raise money, all from voluntary contributions, for this living memorial to Shakespeare and his contemporaries. Wanamaker died before the project was complete, but his ashes lie beneath the stage and his daughter Zoe was the first to speak at its opening in 1997.

## Turn right at the Bear Gardens.

On the corner as you turn you will see the only remaining **ferryman's seat** in the wall of a Greek Restaurant. He sat here while waiting for customers. Legend has it that if a ferryman had a foreigner or country bumpkin in their boat, the fourpence agreed might increase to sixpence midstream – or else.

It's difficult to quantify the least savoury form of entertainment that our ancestors enjoyed, but Bear Baiting must be up there. When a play by Ben Jonson failed to please on its first night, the manager of the Rose Theatre Philip Henslowe said, 'Tomorrow night, we bring the bears in!'. This would guarantee an audience: a tethered bear attacked by mastiff dogs. Queen Elizabeth was said to be highly amused when a dog was flung into the audience onto the lap of the French Ambassador. That of course was the first Queen Elizabeth.

## Turn left along Park Street.

On the left is the site of the **Rose Theatre**. It is still being excavated, but if open do go in. Here the leading actor, Edward Alleyne, was playing Marlowe's Doctor Faustus one night when, as the 'Deadly Sins' appeared, he saw not seven, but eight. He gave up acting that night and with his considerable fortune founded Dulwich College, whose old boys are known to this day as Old Alleynians.

## Walk under the bridge and cross the road.

Here, opposite The Financial Times building is the original site of **The Globe Theatre**, close enough to the Rose for each to hear how their rival's show was being received.

## Turn left at the end of the road, towards the river down Bank End.

Pass Vinopolis, billed as 'London's Wine Tasting Centre' to **The Anchor** pub. Samuel Pepys watched the Great Fire of London in 1666 from what was then a tiny ale-house. Sam Wanamaker brought Michael Caine and Mel Gibson here to encourage them to give money for Shakespeare's Globe.

## Walk under the railway bridge and onto the cobbled Clink Street.

**The Clink** gaol gave rise to one of the many slang terms for prison. If you go inside, be prepared to face screaming, bloodied actors out to scare you witless. To the left are refurbished bonded warehouses and to the right the remains of a great rose window looming above what was once the banqueting hall of the **Bishop of Winchester's Palace**. It was here that a gross and unprepossesing, middle-aged Henry VIII first saw 18 year old Katherine Howard dancing. Pushed by her family, she became his fifth wife, but who could blame her when she found the charms of handsome Thomas Culpepper more to her taste. Well, Henry could, so she paid the ultimate price.

## Emerge from Clink Street into Cathedral Street.

A modern full scale replica of Francis Drake's **Golden Hind** sits in its dry dock. Drake sailed round the world in 1577-80 and four hundred years later this replica did the same. It hosts visits from schools in which children can dress up as Tudor sailors and receive living history lessons about Elizabethan naval history.

## Bear right and go into the churchyard.

The heavily restored **Southwark Cathedral** dates in part back to the Middle Ages. Do go in if you have the time. Shakespeare's actor brother Edmond is buried here. Although funerals then were usually held in the afternoon, the churchwarden's accounts state that he was 'buried with the forenoon toll of the Great Bell... 20 shillings'. This enabled his fellow actors to attend and still make it back to the theatre for their afternoon show. John Harvard, founder of Harvard University, was baptised here in 1607: his mother came from Stratford-upon-Avon so is it fanciful to think that 'old friend of the family' William Shakespeare attended?

## Back in Cathedral Street, dive (right) into the market and wander through to Stoney Street.

**Borough Market** is at its best and busiest from Thursday to Saturday. The oldest market in London - dating back to the 13th century - it is the food lovers' paradise. Fast food from all nations, fresh vegetables, fish and meat, artisan cheeses and ham from acorn-fed pigs. And two rather fine pubs, The Globe Tavern and The Market Porter.

## Walk left up Stoney Street and cross the main road where it forks. Walk right up Borough High Street.

Once packed with inns this is where travellers had to stay if they arrived in London too late to cross London Bridge. Also, if anyone wanted an early start they could stay as Geoffrey Chaucer's Canterbury pilgrims did at The Tabard. Most of the inns were destroyed in 1676, when a devastating fire swept Southwark. **The George Inn** narrowly avoided total destruction. Rebuilt and now, managed by the National Trust, it is London's only surviving galleried coaching inn. The Parliament Bar was the waiting room for coachmen and passengers, the Middle Bar was the Coffee Room, and like so many places in London was a haunt of Charles Dickens.

Stay here for lunch or slip back to Borough Market.

THE JUDGE AND THE SHOWGIRL

# Holborn and Covent Garden

**WALK 7**

A fascinating court case makes good theatre and a bad night at the theatre can be something of a trial. The Inns of Court are close enough to Covent Garden and the West End for the two worlds frequently to collide, as the late 'News of the World' was always keen to point out.

**Start**: Holborn
**Finish**: Covent Garden
**Distance**: 1½ miles (2.4km)
**Refreshments**: Punch and Judy

Entrance to Twinings

## ON THIS WALK

- Lincoln's Inn Fields
- Sir John Soane's Museum
- Hunterian Museum
- Lincoln's Inn
- Temple Church
- The Devereux

42 / WALK 7 – HOLBORN AND COVENT GARDEN

From Holborn station walk left down Kingsway and take the third left along Remnant Street.

You come upon the largest square in London, **Lincoln's Inn Fields**. In medieval times this was used for pasture, jousting, sport and executions. It descended into shabbiness until the 18th century when new houses were built and distinguished, wealthy residents, many of them in the law, lived here. Mr Tulkinghorn, the sinister lawyer in Dickens' 'Bleak House' had offices here.

## Go straight ahead with terraced houses to your left.

**Sir John Soane's Museum** is an Aladdin's Cave. Soane lived here from 1792 to 1837. If you go in, you will notice how he uses natural light throughout the house and every spare corner to contain another treasure. His eccentric collection includes the sarcophagus of Pharaoh Seti I and the 'Picture Room'. Here staff unveil over 100 paintings on hinged screens with the final flourish displaying William Hogarth's 'The Rake's Progress'. If you only visit one museum in London, make it this one.

## Cut straight across the gardens.

Before you reach the bandstand, look back and revel in the glorious mixture of facades, with the dome of the Edwardian Pearl Assurance building in High Holborn looming above them.

The Royal College of Surgeons contains the **Hunterian Museum**. The collection of 18th-century surgeon John Hunter was the first modern pathology collection in Britain. It includes preserved examples of common diseases of the 18th century, the skeleton of Charles Byrne, 'the Irish Giant', and brain of computer pioneer, Charles Babbage.

## Walk left.

The red brick **Land Registry** has details of who owns what land throughout the country and can advise on local house prices too.

## Walk through the gate ahead.

**Lincoln's Inn** was founded in the 14th century and probably named after Thomas Lincoln the 'King's Serjeant' of Holborn, who trained legal apprentices. There are four 'Inns of Court' - Inner Temple, Middle Temple, Gray's and Lincoln's. Anyone who wants to become a barrister and represent a client in a trial must study at one of the four Inns of Court. These Inns were once just that. Young men in medieval times had their accommodation at an Inn, as well as their education.

## Walk straight ahead to the arch opposite.

On your left is the Victorian **New**

| Royal Courts of Justice | Bush House | Waldorf Hotel | |
|---|---|---|---|
| | Twinings | | Aldwych Theatre | Ivor Novello |

WALK 7 – HOLBORN AND COVENT GARDEN

**Hall** and Library. To the right, countless lawyers' chambers with lists of their judges, barristers and clerks beside each door.

## Go under the arch.

This is the oldest part of Lincoln's Inn dating to the 1490s. It was the setting for the Court of Chancery in Dickens' 'Bleak House'. His interminable case of Jarndyce versus Jarndyce was based on 'the Great Jennings Case', a property dispute, that ran throughout his lifetime and beyond for 90 years.

Up the stairs to the left and often open to visitors is the atmospheric chapel.

## Go through the gate and into Chancery Lane and turn right.

The outfitters in Chancery Lane have a target market. Shops selling smart suits for the snappily dressed barrister, then Church's for shoes and Ede and Ravenscroft for 'wigs, gowns and hoods'.

At Fleet Street, look over at the half-timbered house opposite, **Prince Henry's Room**. This is one of the few buildings in The City to survive the Great Fire of 1666. It is named after the eldest son of James I who died before he could become king, so leaving the crown to his younger brother, Charles I.

To its left, what is now Barclays Bank, used to be **'Gosling's Bank'**, one of several private banks that were established in this area. The Gosling's sign with three red squirrels still hangs outside.

## Cross Fleet Street and through the gate into Inner Temple Lane.

The round church on the left is the **Temple Church**. Built in the 12th century by The Knights Templar, it has been intermittently restored through the centuries, especially after it was gutted by incendiary bombs in May 1941. When the Templars were persecuted and stripped of their wealth in 1312, it passed to the Knights Hospitaller of St John who leased it to lawyers. The church had quirky opening hours for years until it became famous worldwide thanks to 'The Da Vinci Code'.

## Go right down Elm Court and through the colonnade, then a jink left and right.

**Middle Temple Hall** was completed in the 16th century and in 1601 saw the first production of Shakespeare's 'Twelfth Night'. If it's not too close to lunchtime ask at the door if you can look inside. It has a double hammer-beam roof and a vast table made from a single piece of oak (8.4 metres long) on a raised dais.

## Leave Middle Temple into Devereux Close.

**The Devereux** is the site of the palace owned of Queen Elizabeth I's ill-starred favourite, Robert Devereux, Earl of Essex. In the early 1700s this was 'The Grecian' coffee house which attracted intellectuals, writers and opposition politicians. Sir Isaac Newton and Edmond Halley were regulars and discussion often became heated. On one occasion two gentlemen drifted into a dispute over the accent on a Greek word. The argument was protracted and at length grew angry. As neither could convince the other they decided to settle the matter outside with swords. After a few passes, one of them was run through the body, and died on the spot.

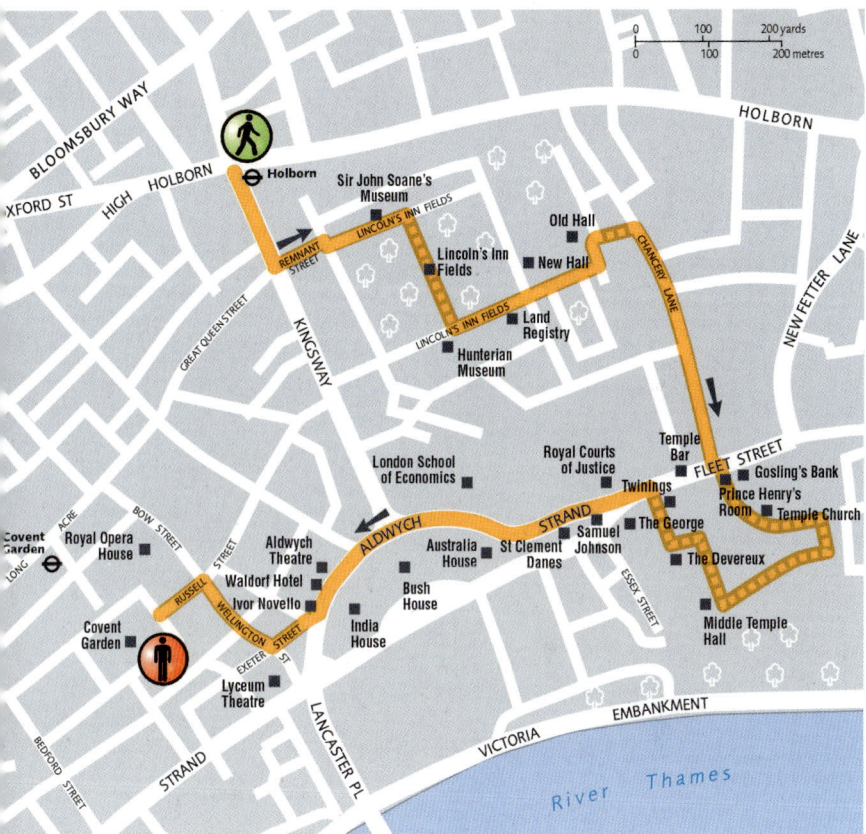

Turn right and follow the alley back to Fleet Street.

**The George** on your left dates back to 1723 in part and is one of the many characterful pubs along the Strand and Fleet Street.

When you reach the main road, look to the right where an angry dragon on top of a column marks the boundary between the cities of London and Westminster. This is where the arch known as **Temple Bar** once stood: too small to cope with 19th-century traffic, it now sits next to St Paul's well away from the road. When the monarch enters the City of London, the Lord Mayor will present the ceremonial sword here; he touches it and command of the city transfers to the crown until he leaves.

**The Royal Courts of Justice** across the road were built by George Street, an architect whose dream was to build a cathedral. Since there were none to build he created this cross between a gothic church and fairy tale castle. This is the centre of Civil Law – land, divorce, libel, appeals, etc. You may recognise the entrance from countless television news bulletins, when winners and losers come out to face the press.

Take the zebra crossing halfway across the road to the back of St Clement Danes Church.

Look back at the entrance to **Twinings**. In 1706, Thomas Twining acquired the taste for drinking tea rather than ale

Shop front in Covent Garden

or coffee at breakfast time and began to sell tea from his coffee house. The first tea drunk in London came from China, but the British later transplanted it to the Indian sub-continent. In 1787 Twinings chose its logo: it is now the oldest commercial logo in continuous use. In 1933 the popular blend 'English Breakfast' was created here.

The statue is to **Samuel Johnson**, the 'man of letters' who lived off Fleet Street where he created the first Dictionary of English. Johnson worshipped here although in his day the walls of the church were not of course scarred by shrapnel as they are now.

### Don't trip over any TV news crews who might be waiting here and walk round the church to the front.

The name **St Clement Danes** is believed to come down from 886 when King Alfred allowed Danish invaders who married local girls to settle and worship here in the 'Ald Wic or Old Settlement', now known as Aldwych.

It was natural that the Danes should dedicate the church to St Clement, patron saint of mariners. Gutted by incendiary bombs in 1941, it was rebuilt to become the home church of the RAF. As part of the rebuilding, a Latin inscription was added over the main door of the church: 'Built by Christopher Wren 1682. Destroyed by the thunderbolts of air warfare 1941. Restored by the Royal Air Force 1958.' It is usually open: inside and outside are memorials and tributes primarily to those who fought in World War II.

### Cross to the other side of Aldwych and walk left.

To your right is London School of Economics and Political Science, better known as **LSE**. Founded in 1895, it retains its individuality although part of the University of London since 1900.

On the island on the left is **Australia House**, home to that country's High Commission. Flanking the entrance are statues representing the Awakening and Prosperity of Australia. Most recently, Oz House played Gringott's Bank in the Harry Potter films.

Next door is **Bush House**. Built in 1919 by American Irving T Bush as a trade centre, in 1940 it became the home of the BBC's Foreign Language World Service until the lease ran out in 2012. The statue representing America lost its left arm in The Blitz. In 1970 an American director of the Indiana Limestone Company visited his daughter at LSE, saw the damaged statue and persuaded the company to send a new arm and a stonemason to attach it, in time for the Silver Jubilee celebrations of Elizabeth II in 1977. You can just make out the join.

## Cross Kingsway.

**India House**, beyond Bush House, has the symbols of Indian states along the wall and on this side of the road, the **Aldwych Theatre**, once the London home of the RSC is the first of many theatres we'll see in what the world knows as 'The West End'.

William Waldorf Astor was one of the richest men in the USA, but a family feud led him to up sticks to London where in 1908 he built the **Waldorf Hotel**. It would look at home in Paris, with its highly decorated pavilion roofs and plush interiors. Astor bought Hever Castle (where Anne Boleyn grew up) and the Cliveden estate in Buckinghamshire, but lost interest in public life, became a recluse and in 1915 passed his business interests to his son: his daughter in law Nancy Astor became Britain's first female MP.

Beyond the Waldorf a blue plaque gives a clue as to why the Strand Theatre has been renamed. **Ivor Novello** made his name in 1914 with the song 'Keep the Home Fires Burning' and went on to write and star in a series of romantic musicals from 'The Dancing Years' to 'King's Rhapsody'. He also played the sinister lead role in Alfred Hitchcock's first, and silent, film, 'The Lodger'.

## Take Exeter Street and turn right into Wellington Street.

The **Lyceum Theatre** nearly went dark forever a few years back but was saved by the long running show, 'The Lion King'. In the late 19th century actor manager Sir Henry Irving and his leading lady, Ellen Terry played all the best parts. On one occasion a young Irish stage manager wrote a play whose main character was based on Sir Henry. The great thespian wasn't impressed, so the young man rewrote the play as a novel. He was Bram Stoker: the novel was 'Dracula'.

## Turn left into Russell Street.

If you don't choose to turn left you will come to the recently refurbished **Royal Opera House** ahead of you, but for food, drink, street entertainment and arty market stalls plunge into London's first square, **Covent Garden**.

Eat and drink anywhere and everywhere, sit in a café, lounge on a step or find peace and quiet in the 'Punch and Judy'.

# THE DUKE OF BEDFORD'S BACK GARDEN

# Bloomsbury

Poets, painters, novelists, education and the British Museum. What more intellectual stimulus might one need? Much of Bloomsbury lies within the Bedford Estate and many names of streets and squares are associated with the Russell family, the Duchy of Bedford.

| Start | Finish | Distance | Refreshments |
|---|---|---|---|
| Euston Square | Russell Square | 2½ miles (3.8km) | British Museum |

Gordon Square

## ON THIS WALK

- 'Catch Me Who Can'
- University College London
- Darwin Building
- Mary Ward Centre
- Foundling Museum
- Dickens Museum

48 / WALK 8 – BLOOMSBURY

**You emerge at a busy junction.**

**Richard Trevithick** harnessed steam power in the tin mines of his native Cornwall. Here, in 1808 he gave the first successful demonstration of the railway engine, charging one shilling for a ride on the 'Catch Me Who Can' on a circular track. Although many were happy to pay for the ride, few came forward to invest. A disappointed Trevithick left for the silver mines of Peru. He returned in 1829 to witness the Rainhill Trials in which George Stephenson heralded the railway age with his 'Rocket'.

## Walk down Gower Street.

On your right are the newer units of **University College Hospital** and Alfred Waterhouse's original red brick UCH just beyond them. This is where George Orwell died of tuberculosis only months after his novel '1984' had become an international success.

## Go through the gates on the left into the courtyard of **University College London** (UCL).

The colonnaded Wilkins Building, named after its architect, once stood proud and alone when UCL was founded in the 1820s. To its left is the Slade School of Art (Richard Hamilton, Rachel Whiteread, Anthony Gormley et al).

UCL was founded in 1828 by Jeremy Bentham, James Mill and others as a non-residential university that welcomed students and lecturers regardless of their religious beliefs - unlike Oxford and Cambridge which only gave degrees to Anglicans. It was dubbed by traditionalists, 'The Godless College on Gower Street' and an Anglican rival, King's College was established on The Strand two years later. Now they are both part of the vast London University.

In 1878 UCL became the first British university to grant degrees to women.

## Walk diagonally across the courtyard to the right-hand corner and enter the foyer of the **South Wing**.

Here you can pay tribute to the mummified form of Jeremy Bentham who bequeathed a large amount of money on condition that his body be preserved and displayed here. Each year Bentham, seated in his own chair in a mahogany case with glass doors, walking stick in hand, is carried to the AGM where he is minuted as being 'present but not voting'.

## Leave the courtyard and continue down Gower Street.

Pass the **Darwin Building** on the left – Charles Darwin lived in a house on this spot while writing 'On the Origin of Species'.

## Turn left down Torrington Place and walk to the corner of Gordon Square.

| Virginia Woolf | | Dorothy L Sayers | | Sylvia Plath | |
|---|---|---|---|---|---|
| | Vanessa Bell | | Ted Hughes | | J M Barrie |

WALK 8 – BLOOMSBURY

The **bookshop** on your right is the idiosyncratic work of Charles Fitzroy Döll, Surveyor to the Bedford Estates in the 1890s.

Here is the **Church of Christ the King**, a fine example of mid-Victorian Gothic revival architecture. Do go in and soak up its High Anglican atmosphere.

## Continue along the left side of the square and cross into the garden opposite Dr Williams Theological Library.

The sculpted head is of the Indian Nobel prize winning poet Rabindranath Tagore, who studied at UCL in 1878. In the far corner, the bust of Noor Inayat Khan, bilingual in French and English, she played in this square as a child, and was parachuted into occupied Paris as a radio operator in 1943. Her resistance cell was infiltrated and she was executed in Dachau aged 30.

**Gordon Square** was developed by Thomas Cubitt in the early 19th century, one of the first builders to employ architects, craftsmen and builders on long-term contracts. Materials were bought in bulk; windows and doors mass produced. Eventually his workshops covered eleven acres (4.45 hectares) of Pimlico.

## Out of the garden gate opposite and note the three plaques.

**John Maynard Keynes** whose economic theories of growth and full employment dominated the Western World from 1945 to the 1970s was a member of the Bloomsbury Group.

**Sir Leslie Stephen** lived at **No. 46** and his daughters Virginia Woolf, the writer, and painter Vanessa Bell, were at the centre of this network of artists, writers and critics, who delighted in 'the pleasures of human intercourse and the enjoyment of beautiful things.'

Farther to the right the house of **Lytton Strachey**, the biographer.

It was said of the 'Bloomsberries' that they were 'couples who lived in squares and loved in triangles': no room here to chronicle all the hanky panky but amidst the love affairs and personal tragedies important art, criticism and literature emerged.

## Walk left and at the top of the square turn right along Endsleigh Place into Tavistock Square.

Straight ahead is the 1925 frontage of the **British Medical Association** (BMA). This is where on 7th July, 2005, the No. 30 bus blew up. There was a 'catastrophe' team in the BMA at the time, which knew enough to wait in case there was a second explosion, but then emerged to deal with the tragedy.

The BMA is built on the site of a house where Charles Dickens lived

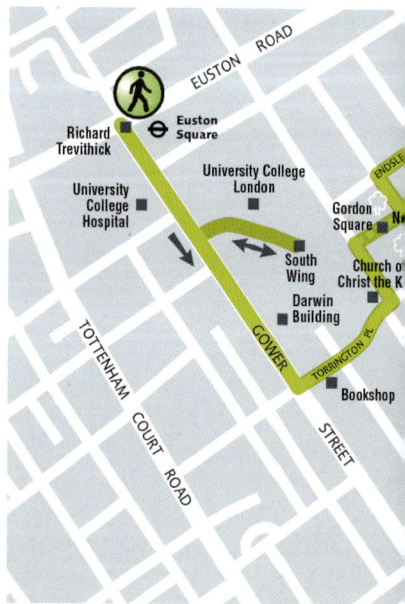

when he wrote 'A Tale of Two Cities' and 'Bleak House', before he jumped ship and left his wife and 10 children for a young actress, Ellen Ternan.

## Go right into the gardens and keep straight on to the far side.

Immediately on your right is the **Memorial Stone** to conscientious objectors who died while acting as stretcher bearers, doctors, ambulance drivers, etc. It was unveiled by Sir Michael Tippett in 1994. Beside it a flowering cherry tree, planted to honour victims of Hiroshima, the first city to be devastated by atomic power in August 1945.

In the middle a statue of **Mahatma Gandhi**, the founding father of independent India, who studied law at UCL and then trained as a barrister at the Inner Temple. The Polish sculptor Fredda Brilliant used an Indian porter from UCL as her model.

The square was built in a unified style like the terrace on your right. All that ended with the bombing of World War II. The modern **Tavistock Hotel** sits four-square on the site of the Hogarth Press founded by Leonard Woolf for his wife Virginia. Its destruction may well have been a contributory element in her suicide in 1941.

## Leave the gardens and head left along Tavistock Place.

**The Mary Ward Centre** on your left is an indefinable building with a grand porch, idiosyncratic guttering and quirkily placed windows. Mary published novels under her married name Mrs Humphrey Ward. Instrumental in setting up the first women's college in Oxford, a pioneer of education for physically disabled children and the play centre movement, she was the first female journalist to visit the trenches in World War I. On her death, she left money to the centre to provide 'cultural and educational opportunities to those denied these through circumstances of birth.'

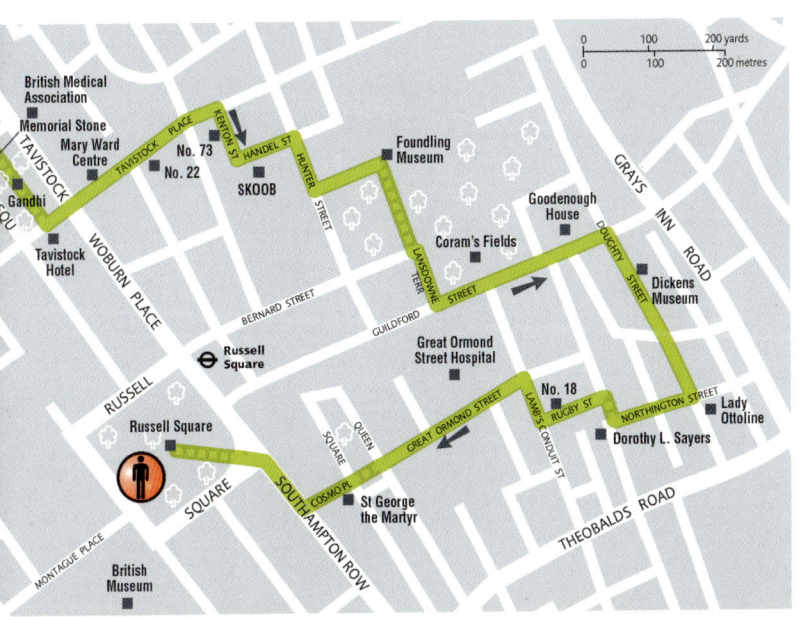

WALK 8 – BLOOMSBURY / 51

Cross at **No. 22** to admire the mosaic step and if you feel the need slip down into the cosy Bloomsbury Coffee House. Then continue until you turn right into Kenton Street.

The print shop at **No. 73** was, as it says, a Building Contactors. Look up and there is the pulley system that could hoist materials to the top floor for safe keeping.

Straight ahead of you is **SKOOB** one of the finest second hand bookshops in London.

Turn left along Handel Street and take the first right. Turn first left to The Foundling Museum.

**The Foundling Museum** commemorates Captain Thomas Coram. Orphaned at 7, after years at sea he made his fortune as a shipwright in Boston, Massachusetts. In 1719 he returned to Rotherhithe for a peaceful retirement, but walking the City on winter mornings became distressed at the number of dead and dying babies abandoned in the streets. It took him 17 years to establish his Foundling Hospital and he never did retire. George Frederick Handel gave benefit concerts to raise money and William Hogarth designed the children's uniforms and decorated the walls with works of contemporary British artists.

Through the gardens and down Lansdowne Terrace turn left along Guilford Street.

You are passing **Coram's Fields** on your left: these are the gates where unwanted babies were left in the 18th century. Now it is a children's playground to which no adult is admitted unless accompanied by a child.

**Goodenough House** is on the left.

This residential centre was founded by Frederick Goodenough to provide a collegiate life along Oxbridge lines for able young men from the Dominions and Colonies, future leaders of the Empire. Currently the community consists of around 650 students and senior scholars from over ninety different countries, many with partners and families.

Keep going and turn right down Doughty Street.

No. 49 on the left is the **Dickens Museum**. Early in his marriage to Catherine Hogarth, Dickens lived here. He doted on Catherine's younger sister, Mary, who one night suddenly developed a fever. Dickens sat with her until she died. She was 17. He wore a locket containing a twist of her hair for the rest of his life. Many a commentator on Dickens and his female characters has pointed out the number of his innocent young beauties who die young, just like Mary.

Keep going and turn right at Northington Street.

The **Lady Ottoline** pub is named after the salon hostess of the Bloomsbury Set, Ottoline Morrell. Nicknamed Lady Utterly Immoral at the time, she was mercilessly lampooned by D H Lawrence in 'Women in Love' as Hermione Roddice.

Past Cockpit Yard.

Salutary to remember that cockfighting was only banned in 1834.

At the corner of St James's Street there is a blue plaque.

**Dorothy L Sayers** was one of the first women to be awarded a degree at Oxford, she cut a dash while at Somerville College, striding down the High, smoking a cigar, with eye-catching earrings and her cloak flowing out behind her.

On graduating, she worked for Benson's Advertising, came up with the slogan, 'My Goodness, my Guinness' and the phrase, 'It pays to advertise'. One of the 1930s 'Queens of Crime' she created the aristocratic sleuth, Lord Peter Wimsey and his wife, Harriet Vane, to whom she gave an address in Doughty Street.

Go right and turn left at The Rugby Tavern (much of the land here is owned by Rugby School), go past Emerald Court (left), the narrowest street in London, and stop outside No. 18.

This house is where the poets Ted Hughes and Sylvia Plath spent the first night of their honeymoon in 1956 before leaving for the unspoilt Spanish fishing village of Benidorm. He chronicled their relationship in his collection, 'Birthday Letters'. In the poem **'18 Rugby Street'**, he says 'It's possessed/Whoever goes into it never gets properly out.' So true. The marriage ended in tragedy six years later when abandoned by Ted, Sylvia took her own life. Some years later his second wife, Assia, did the same. Ted went on to become Poet Laureate.

At Lamb's Conduit Street turn right, then left into Great Ormond Street.

**Great Ormond Street Hospital for Sick Children** was founded in 1851 as the first hospital for children in the country. J M Barrie left all the royalties for 'Peter Pan' to this hospital; when that about ran out, a sequel, 'Peter Pan in Scarlet' was written to offset the loss of revenue.

Continue to Queen Square.

**St George the Martyr** predates the square although it was the Victorians who gave it a zinc steeple. An annual Christmas dinner used to be held here for chimney sweeps' apprentices. It's where Ted Hughes and Sylvia Plath married.

When King George III suffered from porphyria he came here for treatment and his wife Queen Charlotte prepared food in the cellar of the pub now called the Queen's Larder. She served it off pewter plates: unfortunately in those days pewter was an alloy of lead, which did nothing to improve George's health.

Down the paved passage of Cosmo Place and turn right up Southampton Row towards Russell Square. Cross at the lights and make for the fountain in the middle of the square.

Laid out by Sir Humphrey Repton in the early 19th century, **Russell Square** is dominated by Fitzroy Döll's 1898 fairy tale terracotta Russell Hotel. Opposite is the Portland stone Senate House, administrative centre of London University. In World War II it housed the Ministry of Information which censored, among others, the works of George Orwell. As a result he immortalised it as his Ministry of Truth in '1984'.

Have a coffee or lunch in the café in the square or perhaps along Montague Place to the back door of the **British Museum** (BM). As well as being a treasure chest of world culture, the BM has rest rooms, cafeterias and a fine restaurant.

WALK 8 – BLOOMSBURY / 53

# FOR PARLIAMENT?

# Whitehall

**WALK 9**

For over a thousand years Whitehall has been the focus of political, royal and religious power. In the Middle Ages, those who governed the English gravitated 'up west' where the air was sweeter, the fields greener and streets safer.

| Start | Finish | Distance | Refreshments |
|---|---|---|---|
| Charing Cross | Westminster | ¾ mile (1.4km) | The Red Lion |

Admiralty Arch

## ON THIS WALK

Charing Cross — Admiral Lord Nelson — Captain James Cook — Horse Guards Parade — Household Cavalry — Banqueting House

54 / WALK 9 – WHITEHALL

**Come out of Charing Cross mainline station onto the Strand.**

The taxis turn round the **Charing Cross** itself. When Eleanor of Castile, wife of King Edward I, died in Nottinghamshire in 1190, her embalmed body was escorted to Westminster Abbey for burial. In every town the cortège stopped for the night Edward built a cross: this is a Victorian reconstruction of the final Eleanor Cross.

**Turn left along the Strand to the lower side of Trafalgar Square.**

**Admiral Lord Nelson** commanded the victorious British fleet at the Battle of Trafalgar in 1805. He was shot during the engagement and died aboard his flagship HMS *Victory* having been told that the battle was won and that he had prevented Napoleon Bonaparte from invading Britain. Today he stands on top of his column impassive witness to celebrations, marches, concerts, and the hurly burly of everyday life in Trafalgar Square.

To your right adorned with a golden springbok is the **South African High Commission** and beyond it the slender steeple of James Gibbs' 18th-century **St Martin-in-the-Fields**: yes, these were fields back then. At the top of the square stands the colonnaded portico of the **National Gallery**, one of the world's great collections of European Art. The collection is owned by the nation, and so we can enjoy it free of charge.

**Using controlled pedestrian crossings, head for the arch on the other side of the square.**

This is **Admiralty Arch**, the official start of the 'Victoria Memorial', which runs all the way along The Mall to the statue outside Buckingham Palace. The arch was erected in 1910 in memory of his mother by King Edward VII, one of our many philandering kings, known by contemporaries as 'Edward the Caresser'. It has now been transformed into a hotel and private members' club.

Immediately on your left is **The Old Admiralty**, now part of the Foreign Office, which when Britain had an empire was one of the most important ministries. In front stands the great navigator **Captain James Cook**. He charted the coasts of Newfoundland, Hawaii, New Zealand and much of Australia. Thomas Brock, the sculptor, has placed Cook in a heroic pose, with one foot on a coiled rope: Cook would have been the first to point out that no experienced seaman would ever be daft enough to do that on board ship.

**Bear left between a green glass obelisk and the brown brick windowless fortress.**

The obelisk is part of the **Police Memorial**. The brainchild of film director Michael Winner, he was inspired after the death of WPC Yvonne Fletcher, shot in cold blood while policing a protest outside the Libyan Embassy in 1984.

WALK 9 – WHITEHALL / 55

Life Guard of the Household Cavalry, Whitehall

The vast bulk on your left is **The Citadel**. Built in 1941 as a bomb proof bunker for Naval Operations, it was apparently converted in the late 1940s into a nuclear shelter. Rumours abound as to what's inside, whether there are tunnels that lead from it to Downing Street, Buckingham Palace, etc. It must still be there for some reason otherwise why not pull it down? If you're lucky you'll see it in autumn when the Boston Ivy that clothes it turns a glorious shade of red: what you won't see is the grass lawn on the top which was originally grown to confuse the Luftwaffe.

### Walk to the heart of the parade ground and look around you.

This is **Horse Guards Parade**. A great tournament was held here in 1540 by Henry VIII and to this day each year a Guards Regiment troops its colour – its flag – before the Monarch. In 2012 it also hosted the Olympic Beach Volleyball.

What a contrast between the white and terracotta Admiralty and its Citadel extension. There is a small memorial between them to the Naval Divisions who fought as soldiers in The Great War: the main Naval memorials are appropriately in Portsmouth, Devonport and Chatham.

The **Memorial to the five regiments of Foot Guards** stands on the edge of the park. Look from that anticlockwise and there is the white, Italianate **Foreign and Commonwealth Office** (FCO). The architect George Gilbert Scott was given the commission in the 1850s but Lord Palmerston, the Prime Minister, objected to his plans. Scott had in mind a terracotta, gothic fantasy castle. Palmerston wanted something classical. Scott did not favour the classical style, but a job's a job so he knuckled down and produced what the client demanded. He didn't waste his plan for a gothic fantasy castle though: five years later it emerged as the Midland Hotel at St Pancras.

A statue of **Lord Mountbatten of Burma** stands in front of the FCO and to the left, the brown brick houses back onto the gardens of 10, 11 and 12 Downing Street.

### Leave 'Horse Guards' through the arch.

We are leaving the St James's Park, which was once the sole heavily guarded preserve of Royalty. Two mounted guards from the **Household Cavalry** remain on duty each day. They will either have red uniforms with white plumes in the helmets (Life Guards) or blue uniforms with red plumes (Blues and Royals). If these regiments are on active service, the Hussars stand guard. By all means have your photo taken next to the incredibly patient horses. They are Irish Cross Draught horses, known as 'Cavalry Blacks'. There are still

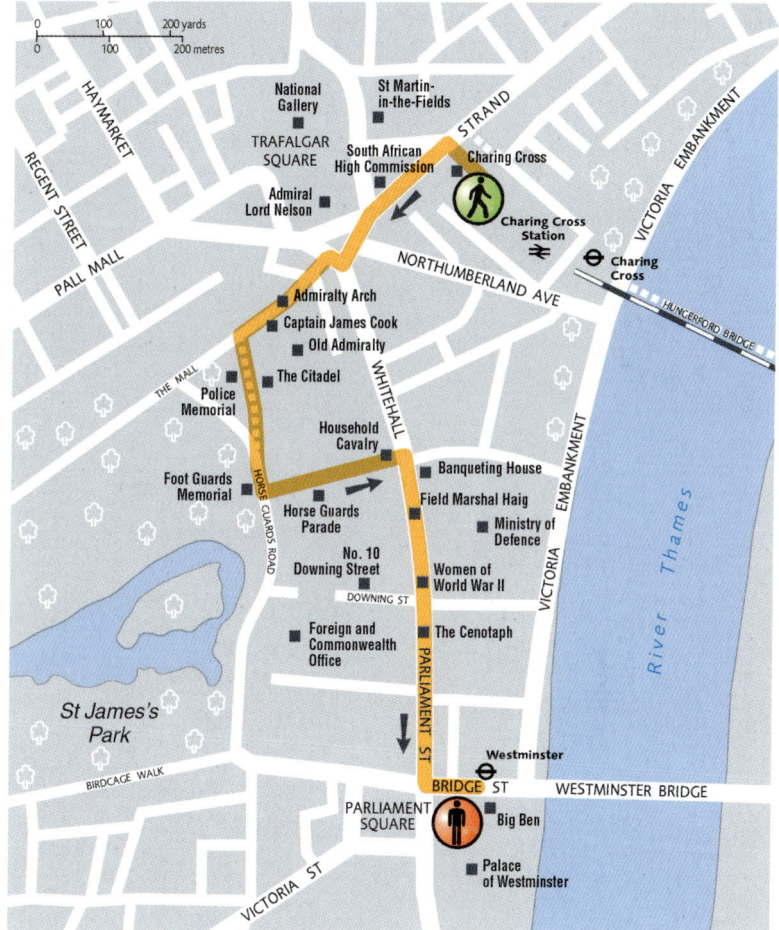

500 war horses in the British Army, but I hasten to add, they are only used for ceremonial purposes.

## You are in Whitehall.

This is the street of government: offices, memorials and ministries all the way. Opposite is Inigo Jones' **Banqueting House**: all that remains of the Whitehall Palace that burnt down in 1698. Throughout the 1640s a bitter civil war was fought in England between the armed forces of Parliament and those of the King. Oliver Cromwell led the Parliamentary army to victory, King Charles I was put on trial for treason and on January 30th 1649 he stepped from these first floor windows onto a wooden platform, whispered a prayer before he paid and pardoned the axeman, who did his job efficiently in one blow. For the next 11 years England was a republic. Look at the clock face over the arch through which you've just passed and pick out a black circle above the Roman numeral II. It was at 2pm that Charles met his fate.

## Turn right down Whitehall. Stay on this side of the road.

In the middle of the road is a mounted statue of **Field Marshal Haig**;

Commander in Chief of British Forces in World War I. Alan Clark's book 'Lions led by Donkeys' pointed the finger and laid the blame for 60,000 British dead in the Battle of the Somme firmly at his door. He ordered them to walk in lines across no man's land under heavy machine gun fire. His reputation has never fully recovered. The establishment were happy for him to take the blame as he was not 'one of us' but came from 'trade'. Although no doubt they were equally happy to drink his family's whisky.

To your left is the imposing **Ministry of Defence** – white with a green roof. Statues of World War II Field Marshals stretch along its length. Slim of Burma, Alanbrooke, chairman of the chiefs of staff, and Montgomery, a figure so familiar, the inscription just says 'Monty'.

The memorial to **Women of World War II** was appropriately unveiled by Queen Elizabeth II who served in the Auxiliary Territorial Service. She drove and maintained vehicles and may well have been the only Head of State in the world who could strip and re-assemble a diesel engine.

## Ahead, **Downing Street** is to your right.

Gone are the days when one was free to walk up to the door of No. 10 and have a picture taken. Margaret Thatcher installed the gates and heavy security in the 1980s. Samuel Pepys described George Downing as the 'greatest rogue in Christendom'. He was sent by Oliver Cromwell to spy on Charles II in France, but became a double agent and on the restoration of the king in 1660 was granted this piece of land on which to build. It is where the First Lord of the Treasury (Prime Minister) has lived since Robert Walpole in the 1740s. When the incumbent loses power, the removal vans slip through from the other end and the old PM is gone in a trice, notes are left, the cat is fed and the new Prime Minister has those inaugural meetings with officials which make clear just how many election promises are still feasible.

## Continue to **The Cenotaph**.

Sir Edwin Lutyens' Cenotaph (empty tomb) is undecorated save for a carved wreath on each end and the words "The Glorious Dead". In 1920 it was erected to commemorate the dead of The Great War, but has become the national focus to commemorate the dead of all subsequent wars, too. The Great War ended at the eleventh hour of the eleventh day of the eleventh month so the monarch leads the tributes on the nearest Sunday each November - Remembrance Sunday.

## Walk on to Parliament Square. Stop on the corner.

You have a fine view of **The Palace of Westminster**. The old palace burnt down in 1834 and Charles Barry, with Augustus Pugin, won the competition to design the new one. The brief was, unlike the Foreign Office, to build in the Gothic Style so that it would harmonise with Westminster Abbey. Major rebuilding works are scheduled at the time of writing and who knows what you will see over the next few years. Traditionally, this is where the two houses of parliament meet. The Commons make laws and the Lords is an advisory chamber. When an act is passed it goes to the monarch as head of state for the Royal Approval. The king is obliged to approve: that was part of the deal when parliament invited Charles II back in 1660.

The Tower overlooking Westminster Bridge is of course **Big Ben**. Or is it? Actually you are looking at the Clock Tower (renamed The Queen Elizabeth II Tower) and Big Ben is the bell inside that tolls the hour. However most people nowadays, apart from the most pedantic, call the tower 'Big Ben'. The present bell is the second to be made. A 16-tonne bell was originally hung and E B Denison, the parliamentarian in charge of the works, put a clapper inside that was heavier than the manufacturer's recommendation. The bell cracked. It was melted down and recast at the Whitechapel Bell Foundry in East London. When this 13½-tonne bell was hung, Denison again ignored the warning about the clapper and cracked this one too. The Foundry was able to mend the crack and the bell was given a half turn on its mount. But listen when Big Ben strikes the hour. The note is meant to be a true 'E', but you can hear that it's slightly off key. Thank you Mr Denison.

Why is it called Big Ben? There are two versions. Either it's named after Benjamin Hall, the Commissioner for Works at Westminster, who was a tall, stout, imposing figure. But many say it's named after the English bare knuckle boxing champion, Ben Caunt. Knowing Londoners, I'd back the latter.

## Westminster Underground Station is on the other side of the street.

For refreshments try The Red Lion a few steps back down Whitehall or St Stephen's Tavern on Bridge Street. There are also plenty of coffee shops here and across the river.

The next walk starts from here, so after lunch…?

*The Clock Tower rises above the Palace of Westminster*

## OR FOR THE KING?

# St James's

**WALK 10**

Not the largest of the Royal Parks, but perhaps the most delightful, St James's Park is the centre piece of this walk. Ancient trees, ubiquitous squirrels and a lake busy with birdlife. Then there are two Royal Palaces, several great houses, and beyond, the world of gentlemen's clubs and shops for the cognoscenti.

| Start | Finish | Distance | Refreshments |
|---|---|---|---|
| Westminster | Green Park | 2 miles (3.2km) | Fortnum and Mason |

The Mall towards the Queen Victoria Memorial

## ON THIS WALK

Westminster Hall | Birdcage Walk | Buckingham Palace
Westminster Abbey | St James's Park | George VI

60 / WALK 10 – ST JAMES'S

At Westminster Station leave by exit 4. Turn right along Bridge Street and cross left at the controlled pedestrian crossing. You have **Winston Churchill** on your right and the clock tower to the left. Keep walking to the statue of **Oliver Cromwell**.

Behind Cromwell stands **Westminster Hall**. Although the old Palace of Westminster burnt down (see walk 9) in 1834, this part of the medieval structure survived. The Hall in its present incarnation dates from the late 14th century and is mainly the work of Henry Yevele. The names of very few master masons have passed down to us, but Yevele has been called the Christopher Wren of the 14th century. Inside, Hugh Herland's oak hammer beam roof has the widest unsupported span in the country. This is where Winston Churchill and Queen Elizabeth II lay in state as thousands came to pay their respects.

Among those tried and condemned here are Sir Thomas More, Queen Anne Boleyn, Guy Fawkes and the man glaring from a niche in St Margaret's Church across the road – King Charles I. His nemesis, Oliver Cromwell, was buried in Westminster Abbey in 1658. Three years later Charles's son returned and had the body disinterred. The head was hacked off and placed on a spike on the roof of Westminster Hall for 25 years. It is now kept safely at Sidney Sussex, Cambridge, his old college.

Retrace your steps to the pedestrian crossing to St Margaret's Church. Cross and turn left. Go through the gate into the churchyard of Westminster Abbey.

On the right is the white Portland stone of St Margaret's – Parliament's church. To your left is **Westminster Abbey**. St Dunstan established a Benedictine abbey here over a thousand years ago, but Henry III rebuilt it as a shrine to Edward the Confessor. Work continued on and off until the time of Henry VII in 1503, when this distinctive end of the church was added in the English Perpendicular style. By that time Europe had started building in the classical style, so this intricate form of the gothic is unique to England.

Walk to the far end of the Abbey.

The Abbey is used for the coronations, royal weddings and funerals. Of all the many tombs of the great and the good inside, including 13 kings and 4 regnant queens, the most important is that of the Unknown Warrior 'buried among the kings because he had done good toward God and toward his house.'

Nicholas Hawksmoor's two 18th-century towers dominate the ceremonial entrance. The niches above the door were never filled, but in the 1990s the Dean and Chapter felt the need to remind tourists that the Abbey was a living Christian church. They commissioned statues of 'Ten

WALK 10 – ST JAMES'S / 61

Christian Martyrs of the Twentieth Century'. In the middle is Martin Luther King, to either side, every continent is represented.

### Cross the Sanctuary towards the pedestrian crossing.

While waiting for a green light, glance down Victoria Street at the round topped column in the distance. This is the neo-Byzantine campanile of Westminster Cathedral, built in the 1890s for the Archbishop of Westminster, spiritual head of England's Roman Catholics.

### Cross Victoria Street and Tothill Street and turn left.

Take note of the plaque on the side of the **Methodist Central Hall** which proved to be one of the stoutest bomb shelters in London. It was in sound enough shape to host the inaugural meeting of the United Nations in 1946.

### At Dartmouth Street turn right.

At the corner with **Queen Anne's Gate** is a pub where the wealthy could hire a Sedan Chair. '**The Two Chairmen**' refers to the strong young men who carried wealthy passengers around London in the 18th century.

### Walk left down Queen Anne's Gate.

Once these were family houses, the earliest dating from 1704. Note the regularity of the new 'Georgian' style of the time: ornamented door hoods, sash windows, wide doors for big dresses and sedan chairs. Notice the upturned cone, a 'snuffer', on the fence of No. 26: a 'link boy' could extinguish his torch here once he'd seen you safely home.

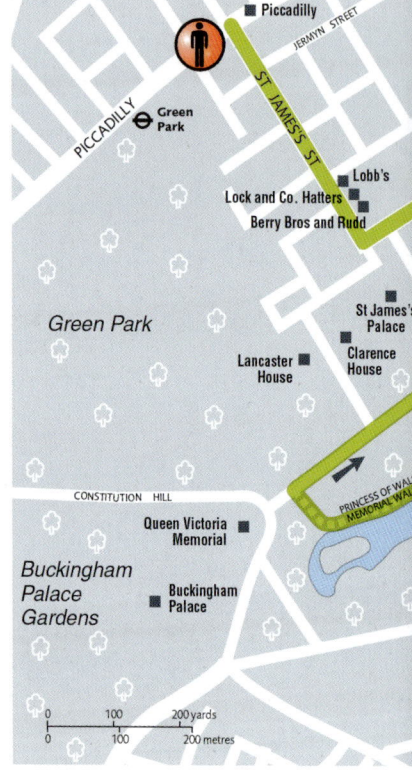

### Turn right at the end of Queen Anne's Gate and cross the road at the lights.

**Birdcage Walk**. James I, and later his grandson Charles II, had cage after cage of songbirds dotted along the walk. An evening stroll to the merry twittering of caged birds away from the hoi polloi. What a glorious thing to be a right-down regular royal king.

### At Queen Anne's Gate bear left across St James's Park towards the bridge over the lake.

Don't trip over the packs of European schoolchildren, the highlight of whose trip to London involves photographing squirrels. At the bridge is a fine view of Buckingham Palace to the left and the London Eye looming over Horse

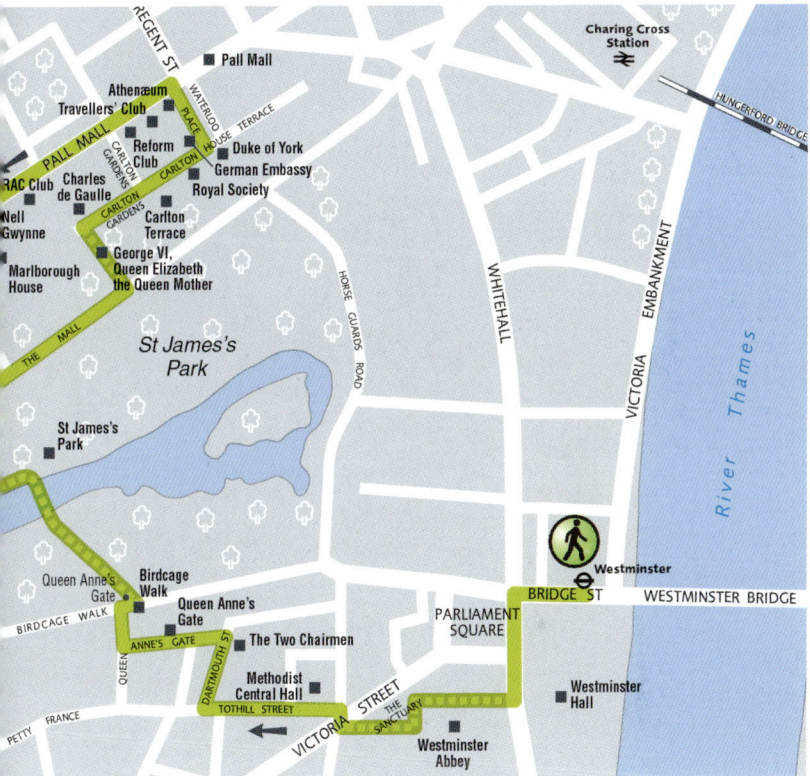

Guards to the right.

**Turn left after the bridge and follow the Princess of Wales Memorial Walk to where it takes you up the hill to the front of Buckingham Palace.**

There are all sorts of water birds. Look carefully and you may see black Australian swans or pelicans which have been here since the Russian Ambassador gave four as a diplomatic gift to Charles II in the 1680s. You will certainly spot the ubiquitous Canada goose: if you're Canadian, please take a couple home with you!

**Buckingham Palace** is official residence of the monarch. The Royal Standard will be flying if the king's at home: otherwise the Union Flag denotes his absence. Originally built in the early 1700s as a country home and bought by George III in 1762, it became the official Royal residence when Queen Victoria moved here in 1837. Ten years after her death the **Queen Victoria Memorial** was unveiled. Carved from a single block of marble, she keeps an eye on The Mall, surrounded by what Osbert Sitwell waspishly called 'tons of allegorical females in white wedding cake marble'. Above them a gold leaf covered Victory rises above the figures of Courage and Constancy.

**Cross the Mall at the lights and walk along the north side away from the Palace.**

Pass **Lancaster House**, used by the Foreign Office for entertaining, and then the white stone **Clarence House**. Guards should be on duty here as

WALK 10 – ST JAMES'S / 63

this is another of the king's London homes. Continue alongside the wall of red-brick **St James's Palace**, built by Henry VIII 500 years ago and last used by Queen Anne until her death in 1714. Her close friend Sarah Churchill, Duchess of Marlborough, built the vast **Marlborough House** next door. It is now the Commonwealth Secretariat. Test your knowledge by identifying all the countries by their flags: to help you they are in alphabetical order.

Then the statues of **George VI and Queen Elizabeth, the Queen Mother** tower above you. The Queen Mother's life spanned the 20th century, but for half of that time she was a widow. Her husband was the second son and dutifully but reluctantly became king on the abdication of his brother. He led the country during World War II. With his simplicity and diffidence, he was an important balance to the flamboyant Winston Churchill. The bas reliefs on either side of the statues show the Royal family during the war and on the other side, the Queen Mum's great love – horse racing.

Before we leave The Mall, look at the impressive swathes of stucco faced houses with Doric columns ahead of you. **Carlton Terrace** was to be the final part of the ceremonial route from Marylebone Park, renamed Regent's Park, down Regent Street to Carlton House where, guess who, the Prince Regent was to live. His favourite architect, John Nash, planned the route but it was never finished, as the Prince practically bankrupted the country with this particular tilt at immortality.

## Take the steps past the statues into Carlton Gardens bearing right along Carlton House Terrace.

The statue of **Charles de Gaulle** and plaques in French and English indicate that in World War II he had his Free French headquarters here. He was the only high ranking French officer active in the cause of the Allies although his relationship with both Churchill and Roosevelt was acrimonious.

## Continue beyond the statue of Lord Curzon, to the Royal Society.

The **Royal Society of London for Improving Natural Knowledge**, known simply as the Royal Society, was granted a Royal Charter by King Charles II in 1660. To become a fellow – FRS – is the highest honour for any scientist. The roll call of past Presidents includes Christopher Wren, Isaac Newton, Joseph Banks, Lord Kelvin, Ernest Rutherford and Howard Florey.

## We come to Waterloo Place (Lower Regent Street).

The house on the corner was the **German Embassy** until 1939. In the early 1930s, the Ambassador was the very popular Leopold von Hoesch. On his death he was replaced by a Nazi, Joachim von Ribbentrop until the embassy was closed in 1939. Von Hoesch had an adored little terrier called Giro. Under the tree next to the house is its grave – Giro – Ein Treuer Begleiter - A True Companion.

At the top of the 38-metre column, the Prince Regent's brother the **Duke of York** surveys St James's Park. It is said he was put so high to keep him away from his creditors. He owed £2 million at the time of his death in 1827.

## Turn away and walk up Waterloo Place.

On the corner with Pall Mall is the **Athenæum** Club, with figures from Parthenon skipping along above the dado. Most members of the Athenæum are professionals concerned with science, the arts and academia. Each 'Gentlemen's Club' in Pall Mall attracts a certain type of clientele.

Go left along Pall Mall.

**Pall Mall** is named from the game 'paille-maille'. This involved driving a ball with a mallet through an iron ring. In 1661 Samuel Pepys wrote in his diary, 'To St James's Park, where I saw the Duke of York playing at Pelemele, the first time that I ever saw the sport'.

First club on the left is the **Travellers' Club** established for gentlemen who had travelled abroad and diplomats posted in London; the **Reform Club** for those who supported parliamentary reform, whence Phileas Fogg went round the world in 80 days; the colonnaded **RAC Club** founded for enthusiasts in the early days of motoring.

There are many blue plaques along this street but the most distinctive is that for **Nell Gwynne**. 'Pretty, witty Nell' - actress and close personal friend of King Charles II. It is the only plaque in London that doesn't explain why we should remember her.

Bear right into St James's Street taking the right-hand pavement.

**Berry Bros and Rudd** have been trading for over 300 years, created Cutty Sark Whisky and have vast cellars stretching under Pall Mall.

In 1850 **Lock and Co. Hatters** produced a domed hat, hardened with shellac, for William Coke, a Norfolk farmer, to protect his gamekeepers'

Berry Bros and Rudd

heads from low hanging branches. Known by Lock's as the 'Coke' it is better known to us by the name of the hatter who made the prototype, one Thomas Bowler. Americans call it the 'Derby' from its association with the classic horse race.

**Lobb the Bootmakers** keep the lasts of every foot they've fitted. A pair of shoes will pass through the hands of 9 different craftsmen and a simple pair of leather shoes won't give you much change from £4,000.

At the top of the road turn into **Piccadilly**.

If you want to take tea at The Ritz it's advisable to book. Farther down towards Hyde Park Corner is the original Hard Rock Café. Otherwise Fortnum and Mason to the right is worth a visit as are many of the small cafés and tea shops all along this once fashionable street.

There are buses in both directions and it is but a step to Green Park station.

## WE NEVER CLOSED

# Soho

**WALK 11**

For much of the 20th century Soho was London's red light district with late night drinking clubs, 'adult entertainment' and the whiff of danger. Though much tidied up, it still has a raffish air and remains what some call a mainstream exotic destination. Now thanks partly to the strong Italian presence, it has some of the finest restaurants and coffee bars in England.

| Start | Finish | Distance | Refreshments |
|---|---|---|---|
| Tottenham Court Road | Piccadilly Circus | 1½ miles (2.3km) | A dim sum lunch in Chinatown |

Wardour Street as Italy melds into Chinatown

## ON THIS WALK

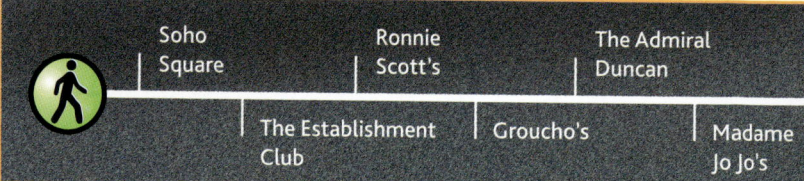

- Soho Square
- The Establishment Club
- Ronnie Scott's
- Groucho's
- The Admiral Duncan
- Madame Jo Jo's

From Tottenham Court Road station take the south side exit on Oxford Street, walk left and then left down Soho Street.

On your right, note the Radha Krishna Temple and its legendary vegetarian restaurant, Govinda's.

Pass straight into Soho Square to the crumbling statue of Charles II.

**Charles II** had many children, but his wife had none. 'So-Ho!' was the hunting cry of his eldest illegitimate son, the Duke of Monmouth, who was among the first to build a mansion here: his house, along with all the others, was demolished in the 18th century as the area declined during the development of more fashionable Piccadilly and Mayfair.

Pass the half-timbered park keeper's hut, bear left as you leave the gardens and walk down Greek Street.

Greek Street was once Hogs Lane, until in the 17th century Greek refugees settled here and built an Orthodox Church, long since gone. It is the street in which **Casanova** stayed on his visit to London in 1764: no doubt he explored the delights Soho had already begun to offer.

At No. 1 Greek Street the House of St Barnabas has supported the homeless for over 160 years. Just beyond it is Noble Rot, formerly the **Gay Hussar** restaurant founded by Victor Sassie in 1953. A half Swiss, half Welsh native of Barrow-in-Furness, Sassie specialised in Hungarian cuisine – goose and goulash – and so could be considered an archetypal mongrel Soho resident. The Hussar was a favourite eating place for three generations of socialist MPs.

Behind **The Pillars of Hercules** leading to Foyles' Bookshop is Manette Street, where, in Dickens' 'A Tale of Two Cities' Dr Manette found peace after years of suffering in The Bastille.

In the early 1960s a generation of satirists burst onto the national scene via the Edinburgh Festival. Peter Cook (see the plaque) created **'The Establishment Club'** at **No. 18** and simultaneously bankrolled the magazine 'Private Eye'. It was a private club, because at that time the Lord Chamberlain could censor any public theatrical performance. Cook had carte blanche to bring comedians as diverse as Lenny Bruce and Barry Humphries to London and poke fun at the very people after whom the club was named. He soon moved on and the club folded in 1964. 'Private Eye' dealt with stories that no mainstream newspaper dared touch, and although it is constantly being sued, has outlived 'The Establishment' by half a century.

On the other side of the road is **L' Escargot**. The plaster bust above the door shows founder, M. George Gaudin, riding a snail. He farmed snails in the basement kitchen, thus making it the first restaurant in Britain to serve fresh 'escargots'. And maybe the last! The restaurant itself is hung with original works by Miro and Chagall.

## Turn right into Old Compton Street, past The Prince Edward Theatre and right again into Frith Street.

On your right is **Bar Italia**. All Italians in the UK were interned during World War II, but in the late 1940s many returned to Soho. This return coincided with the arrival of Achille Gaggia's patented espresso machine. Thus began the coffee revolution.

Bar Italia, run by the third generation of the Polledri family, was founded in 1949. From its earliest days it has acted as a social centre for the Italian community. People who had lost touch with family members during World War II could discover their fate: an unemployed barista might get help from other waiters to find a job. Bar Italia's design was state of the art and the Polledri family have been careful to keep the detail and the continuity of the original. Red and white formica is an important part of the bar; the Gaggia coffee machine has been there for over fifty years; the big screen shows the latest matches in 'Serie A'. Bar Italia retains the atmosphere of a classic Italian café and may it long continue so to do.

Opposite is **Ronnie Scott's**, the spiritual home of British jazz. Anybody who was anybody played here. Ella Fitzgerald, Miles Davis, Count Basie... Ronnie was the compere, famous for his bad jokes, but he was also a fine saxophonist. Listen to The Beatles' 'Lady Madonna' and that's him playing the sax solo.

## Walk left down Bateman Street and into Dean Street.

To your right at No. 28, Peppino Leoni established **Quo Vadis** in 1926 and turned it into one of London's finest restaurants. When Westminster decided to put a blue plaque to Karl Marx on the wall he was furious. 'My clientele is rich people, nobility and royalty and Marx wanted to get rid of them all'. The outside has been delicately refurbished in the style of Charles Rennie Mackintosh.

**Karl Marx** lived here for six years while writing 'Das Kapital'. Conditions were appalling and three of the little Marx children died. Although Eleanor, born here in 1855, went on to become an activist and suffragette.

## Left down Dean Street.

For years, No. 41 was **The Colony Room**, whose most famous member was the artist Francis Bacon. This was Soho's most notorious private drinking club in the 1950s. Founded by the foul mouthed Muriel Belcher, at her death it was passed on to the even more waspish Ian Board. He too has left us now.

At No. 45 is **Groucho's**, a private members club open to men and women, formed in 1985. It takes its name from Groucho Marx's remark that he would never join a club that would have him as a member. Dreamt up by a group of publishers as an alternative to stuffy gentleman's clubs of Pall Mall, it soon became the de rigueur watering hole for those who work in what the Groucho website calls 'the creative industries'.

Across Old Compton Street is **The French House**, a much older haunt of artists and writers. Charles de Gaulle used it as a meeting place for his Free French in the Second World War and in the 1950s it became popular with

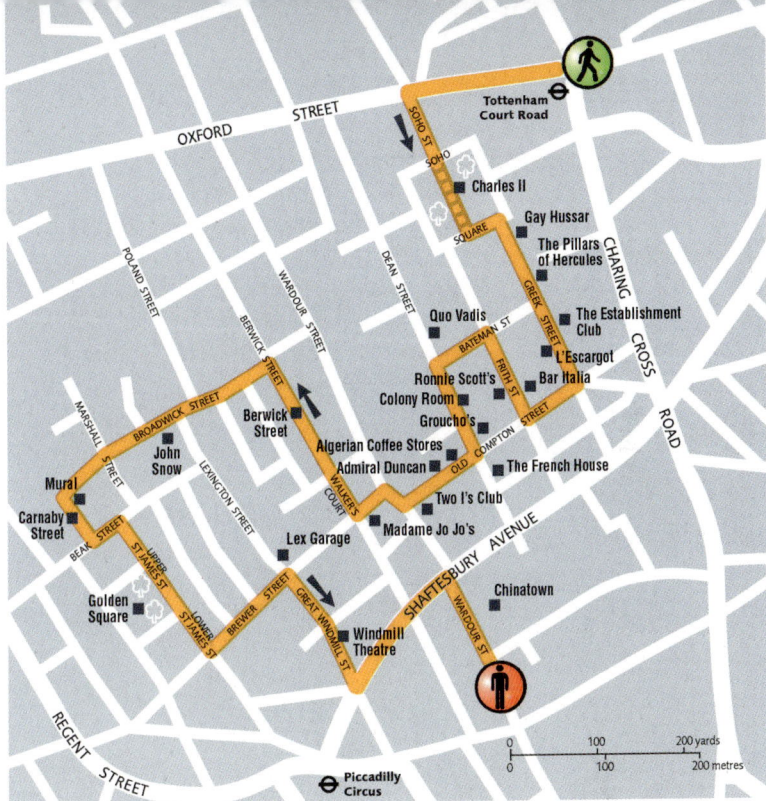

artists Lucien Freud and Francis Bacon, before they headed for The Colony Club. Glance across at it and then…

Turn right along Old Compton Street.

**The Algerian Coffee Stores** established in 1887 by Mr Hassan to sell coffee beans and train people in 'coffee skills'. Today they sell over 80 coffees and 123 teas.

Back in 1953, the poet, Dylan Thomas accidently left the only manuscript of his radio drama 'Under Milk Wood' in **The Admiral Duncan**, just before he went to America. This started a treasure hunt around all the many pubs that Thomas had visited that day. He recorded a staged reading in New York but didn't live to hear the classic BBC version, with Richard Burton. It has for many years been a predominantly gay pub. In 1999, the reclusive Nazi sympathizer, David Copeland, began a series of murderous attacks in Brick Lane against the Bangladeshi community and later here. His nail bomb, left in the bar, killed three and injured many.

On the other side of the road next door to Camisa and Son is a plaque.

The **Two I's Club**, named for its founders the Irani brothers, has a perfect right to be considered the birthplace of British Rock and Roll. In the mid-1950s Lonnie Donegan's rasping voice and skiffle music heralded a new dawn. 'Teenagers' as they were now called came here to drink frothy coffee, hand jive to the tunes of Lionel Bart and scream at sub-Elvis singers, such as Tommy Hicks and Harry Webb - better known as Tommy Steele and Cliff Richard.

Carnaby Street

market since 1688. It hit its stride in the 19th century and still seethes with robust life.

As Berwick Street meets Broadwick Street, turn left. Continue across Poland Street.

The **John Snow** pub is named after the local GP who discovered the cause of cholera. Contemporaries believed that cholera was transmitted in the air, but in 1854, a new outbreak occurred in Soho. After careful investigation Snow was able to identify a water pump in Broadwick Street as the source of the outbreak. This confirmed his belief that cholera was caused by drinking polluted water. He had the handle of the pump removed, and cases of cholera immediately began to diminish. The pump here today is not the original but has been put there to commemorate Snow's achievement: more suitable than the pub, as he was a teetotaller.

Turn right up Wardour Street and immediately left into Brewer Street.

This corner was once the home of burlesque, – dominated by Raymond's Revue Bar, see the neon signs above, and **Madame Jo Jo's**. Both are now closed. Young performers in the tradition of Lily Savage and Danny La Rue must cut their teeth elsewhere. Such is progress!

Cut through Walker's Court (right) and straight ahead up Berwick Street.

In Walker's Court you may be encouraged to enjoy exotic dancing, get a new tattoo or visit an adult bookshop. **Berwick Street** has hosted Soho's

Continue across Marshall Street to Carnaby Street and turn left.

The vast **mosaic mural** on the corner may remind you of where you've walked and what you've seen although its purpose is more to entertain than illuminate.

**Carnaby Street** is where 'Swinging

London' began. In 1960, a young Glasgow tailor called John Stephen set up 'His Clothes' aimed at the new 'mod' generation. 'I Was Lord Kitchener's Valet', 'Kleptomania', 'Lord John' and other stores followed as the street blossomed into a colourful 24-hour carnival for 'dedicated followers of fashion'. The Yardbirds, Kinks and Small Faces helped spread the word and by 1967 Stephen was known as 'The King of Carnaby Street'. Before he died in 2004, he said, 'I was the same age and into pop music, so I gave kids something they could wear to complement that.' Sadly Carnaby Street is now a pale, tacky shadow of what it once was.

**At the plaque to John Stephen, turn left along Beak Street and immediately right down Upper St James Street.**

**Golden Square** has seen better days too. Its decline paralleled that of Soho Square and it also has a crumbling statue of a king at its heart, George II in this case. In Victorian times, Golden Square had become so unprepossessing that Charles Dickens considered it an appropriately dingy place for the evil Ralph Nickleby to live.

**Walk down Lower St James Street and turn left along Brewer Street.**

At the corner of Great Windmill Street enjoy the bright yellow art-deco multistorey car park with its domed tower. Built in 1929 as the **Lex Garage**, it was convenient for theatregoers, and space limitations suggested the solution of parking cars on four levels. Separate rooms were provided for chauffeurs and changing rooms for ladies.

## Walk down Great Windmill Street.

In the 1930s, theatre manager Vivian van Damm introduced a programme of continuous variety at **The Windmill Theatre**. This only took off when, inspired by the Folies Bergère, he put glamorous nude females on stage. As long as they didn't move, they were considered artistic and legal in the eyes of the Lord Chamberlain.

The Windmill proudly boasted that during World War II it never closed, much to the relief of the thousands of servicemen from all over the world waiting for D-Day. After the war it presented a steep learning curve to young comedians like Tony Hancock, Peter Sellers, Bruce Forsyth and Tommy Cooper who had to try out their acts to a stony-faced audience of men waiting for the girls to come back on.

**Down to Shaftesbury Avenue, turn left past four theatres then right into Wardour Street. On your left is the official gate into Chinatown.**

**Chinatown** is a thriving community. The East India Company traded with China from the 17th century and soon after the Chinese began to settle near the docks in East London. Badly bombed during World War II, they bought up cheap properties in Soho. Now everything here is Chinese, right down to the road signs and New Year celebrations.

What else is there to suggest but a dim sum lunch?

ONLY £400 ON THE MONOPOLY BOARD

# Mayfair

**WALK 12**

The annual May Fair authorised by King Edward I was held on the banks of the Tyburn, but in the 18th century Mayfair became a favourite residential area for those who wanted to live close to the King. Once those residents got a toe-hold they banned the May Fair saying that it was much too raucous and lowered the tone.

| Start | Finish | Distance | Refreshments |
|---|---|---|---|
| Green Park | Green Park | 2¼ miles (3.7km) | The Bunch of Grapes |

The Burlington Arcade

## ON THIS WALK

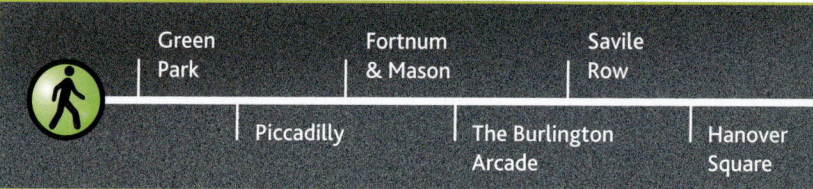

Green Park — Piccadilly — Fortnum & Mason — The Burlington Arcade — Savile Row — Hanover Square

Emerge on the south side of Piccadilly.

**Green Park**, used in the Middle Ages as a burial ground for lepers, was enclosed by Henry VIII as a royal hunting park in the early 1500s. In 1749 several buildings were burnt down during a Royal Fireworks display for George III. In 1814 at a gala for his son, the Prince Regent, the 'Temple of Concord', built especially for the occasion, also exploded during the fireworks. Since then no building has been erected in the park.

## Walk right.

**Piccadilly**, once Portugal Street in honour of Catherine of Braganza, the wife of Charles II, is so called because in the early 18th century, a fashionable starched stiff collar known as a 'picadil' was manufactured here by Robert Baker. This is the southern boundary of Mayfair.

On your right is the **Ritz Hotel**. Built by Cesar Ritz and opened in 1906 in a style classified as Belle Époque-Neoclassical Edwardian - so now we know!

Caruso, Diaghilev, Pavlova, Fairbanks and Chaplin all stayed here in its heyday, when Cesar Ritz retained a man at the entrance whose sole task was to ring a bell if royalty approached. On 28 January 1999 it was chosen for the first public appearance together of the then Prince Charles and Camilla Parker-Bowles, at her sister's birthday party.

**Fortnum & Mason**, London's most prestigious foodstore, was founded in 1707 by William Fortnum (footman to Queen Anne), who raised the capital by selling partially used candles from St James's Palace. He then teamed up with his landlord John Mason to sell groceries to the gentry. Queen Victoria paid for food parcels to the troops in Crimea in the 1850s: these included a 250lb consignment of beef tea requested by Florence Nightingale. Fortnum's also launched Heinz products in this country, most notably Baked Beans in 1895.

**Hatchard's** is the oldest bookstore in London. John Hatchard opened his bookshop here in 1797, inscribing on a plate in the window – 'God blessed my industry and good men encouraged it'. When 18-year-old Noel Coward was caught putting books into a suitcase, he said, 'Really, how badly this shop is run! I could have made off with a dozen books and nobody would have noticed.' He left without any further bother.

## Retrace your steps a little to Fortnum's.

Across the road, Burlington House has been home to the **Royal Academy of Arts** since 1834. It is the sole survivor of the 18th-century mansions which once stood cheek by jowl along this side of Piccadilly. The RA Summer Exhibition in June is open to all comers and each year over 10,000 works are submitted of which about 1,300 are selected for the show. For the rest of the year it hosts high profile one-off exhibitions.

**Cross the road, turn left to reach the arcade on the right and walk through.**

Lord George Cavendish built **The Burlington Arcade** in 1819 to prevent passers-by throwing rubbish into his garden. It's a haven from the Piccadilly traffic with its red carpet and selection of luxury goods, many of which sit arrogantly in the windows with no price tag, as if to say, 'If you need to ask the price, you can't afford me.' Uniformed beadles patrol the arcade to discourage unruly behaviour. They have the authority to eject anyone who runs, carries large packages, opens an umbrella, whistles, hums or sings. The upper floor was once known for 'assignations' and Virginia Woolf wrote that once 'young women could not stray into the crocodile infested swamp that was the Burlington Arcade without their mothers'.

The far end of the arcade is not as fancy owing to the attentions of a Second World War bomber, but at last we are in Mayfair itself. Kensington and Chelsea have become more fashionable over the past fifty years: Mayfair residents being cruelly stereotyped as 'elderly colonels and widows'. It is now on the way up again, as high achieving young foreigners have begun to buy their London pieds-à-terre here.

**Turn left along Burlington Gardens and right up New Bond Street.**

Cartier, Chanel, Ralph Lauren, Tiffany and more: this is the centre of haute couture in London.

**Go right along Clifford Street and left up Savile Row.**

The term 'bespoke suit' originated in **Savile Row**, and this still is the 'golden mile of tailoring'. Pass Richard James, Ozwald Boateng, Issey Miyake, and then as if to say, 'It's all just a bit too male', two Vivienne Westwood shops.

**Turn left along Conduit Street then right up St George Street.**

As you turn the corner you encounter Sotheby's Auction Rooms, dating from 1744 and one of the world's leading auction houses for art.

**St George's**, Hanover Square, was built by John James to serve this fashionable new residential area in 1725. It was the first London church to have a portico, which unapologetically blocks the pavement. The composer George Frederick Handel worshipped here; Percy Bysshe Shelley married Mary Godwin; and Benjamin Disraeli and George Eliot also married at St George's, but not each other. It is this church Alfred Doolittle refers to in the song 'Get me to the Church on Time'.

**Carry on up St George Street.**

Now almost permanently congested with traffic, **Hanover Square** was laid out in 1714 in honour of the new king, George I, Elector of Hanover. Only a few original houses remain, to the left as you enter the square.

On the right once stood the **Hanover Square Rooms**, where J C Bach and Josef Haydn premiered many works. It was also the venue for the 'Dandies' Ball' in 1813. Beau Brummell, the leader of dandy fashion, had fallen out with the Prince Regent, so did not invite him to the ball. But 'Prinnie' came all the same: on arrival he cut Brummell dead and passed on to greet Lord Alvaney, which prompted Brummell to ask Alvaney in a stage whisper, 'Who's your fat friend?' It was the beginning of the end of Brummell's life in society, his debts spiralled and he moved to France where he died penniless and insane.

### Turn left along Brook Street and cross New Bond Street.

Immediately after Lancashire Court, the plaque above **No. 23** heralds one of the jolliest juxtapositions in London. Jimi Hendrix and George Frederick Handel. One can only imagine what they'd have made of each other. Handel House is a museum, but Jimi just gets a plaque.

**Claridge's Hotel**. Founded by former butler William Claridge in 1855, Winston Churchill used it during World War II for secret meetings with US Intelligence. When, against his expectations, he lost the 1945 election, this provided him with a bolt hole.

### Cross Davies Street and continue along Brook Street.

The Grosvenor family were created Dukes of Westminster in 1874 and today, 'Grosvenor Estates' are the richest urban landlords in England with a great deal of land on long term leases. **Grosvenor Square** is at the heart of their property portfolio.

### At Grosvenor Square go into the garden.

The understated oak and granite memorial is to the **British victims of 9/11**. The flowers are carefully chosen and the words 'Grief is the Price we Pay

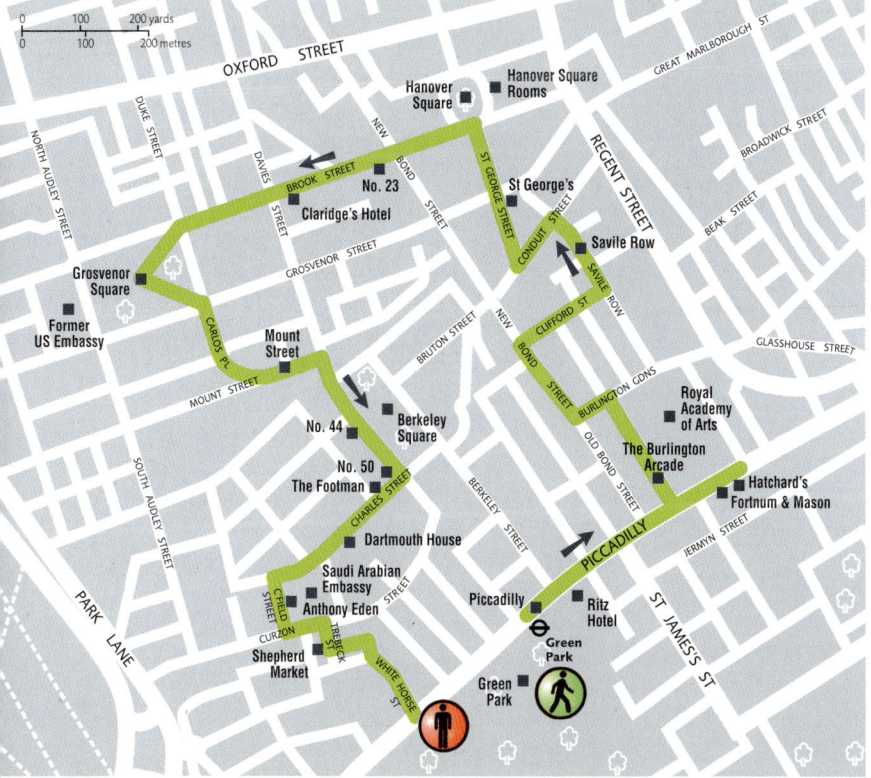

WALK 12 – MAYFAIR / 75

for Love' are from Colin Murray Parkes, a psychiatrist who worked closely with Dame Cicely Saunders in the hospice movement and bereavement counselling.

The square used to be dominated from the far end by the monolithic, **US Embassy.** This fine example of Neo-brutalism has at the time of writing been bought for development by a Qatari real estate company. The present US Embassy is south of the river at Nine Elms**.** In the 1950s, the United States Government purchased this bomb damaged patch of land on a 999 year lease. One of the first visitors was John F Kennedy who remarked that the US owned the land on which all US embassies are built, apart from the one in London. He asked the Duke of Westminster if they could buy the freehold. The Duke replied, 'Yes, in return for the land the US government seized from my ancestors in the 1770s, which, by the way, covered most of Florida, including Cape Canaveral.'

The statue of Franklin Roosevelt on the right looks over to that for the Eagle Squadron, 244 American volunteers who flew in the Battle of Britain while the USA was still neutral.

## Leave along Carlos Place, turn left along Mount Street to Berkeley Square.

**Mount Street**, beyond the Connaught Hotel, has a pink terracotta terrace of apartments with shops at street level, dating from the 1880s. These represent the style favoured by the first Duke of Westminster for his Mayfair Estate.

**Berkeley Square** was originally laid out in the 1730s and the magnificent London plane trees are said to date from 1789.

## Walk down the right-hand side.

**No. 44** houses one of the most exclusive private gambling clubs in London, **The Clermont**. In the 1970s, it acquired a less than wholesome

Nymph statue by Alexander Munro, Berkeley Square

reputation. Member, Lord 'Lucky' Lucan, attempted to murder his wife at home in 1974 but killed the children's nanny instead. It's believed that members of the club spirited him out of the country to East Africa, where he lived out the rest of his life well protected by the expatriate community.

The decorative staircase takes you to the basement and the exclusive club **Annabel's**.

**No. 50**, is said to be the most haunted house in London. It seems that a 'Something or Other', very terrible indeed, haunts a particular room. Apparently one nobleman, brave enough to show that there was nothing to fear, decided to spend the night in the haunted bedroom. His friends found him rigid with fear, eyes bulging from their sockets and unable to speak. He died shortly after.

## Take Charles Street to the right.

On your right is **The Footman**. This post was a fine job for a fit young man who ran in front of his master's carriage through the London streets, in full livery, to clear the way. The footmen had to be healthy, 6-foot tall and attractive: they were noted as the best sources of all the gossip. As the tradition died out, one of the last footmen bought the pub to cater for his friends.

The distinctive **Dartmouth House**, built as the English Speaking Union to promote Anglo-American friendship, bills itself as 'an ideal venue for superior events, from small meetings to large conferences, intimate banquets to gala dinners and private parties to weddings'.

## Turn left down Chesterfield Street.

How ironic that Prime Minister **Anthony Eden** should have lived in the same house as Beau Brummell. Eden, a dapper dresser, known to political enemies in the 1930s as a 'glamour boy', was hardly in the same league as Brummell. In this house the Prince Regent would like to watch the Beau dress and study the way he tied his cravat. That of course was until the unpleasantness at the Hanover Rooms. Eden's career ended unhappily too after he misjudged events in 1956 during the Suez Crisis.

## Turn left along Curzon Street.

Pass the **Saudi Arabian Embassy**, but do not linger. If you do, armed police might move you along.

## Turn right down Trebeck Street.

**Shepherd Market** is on the site of the original May Fair which was a bawdy affair banned in 1708 because of 'disturbances', after which in 1735 Shepherd Market was built and named after its designer, Edward Shepherd.

In the 1920s it became fashionable with Noel Coward, Nancy Cunard and society butterflies of 'The Lost Generation'. Their defiant toast was 'For King and Cocktails!' Since then the market has kept an off colour reputation as centre of the Mayfair sex industry. It retains a louche masculine atmosphere with cigar shops, gun shops and cobblers: everything a country gentleman might wish for.

There are cafés, restaurants, The Market Tavern for refreshment; otherwise take White Horse Street to Piccadilly and turn right for the Hard Rock Café or left to the Ritz!

## A PARK FOR ALL SEASONS

# Hyde Park

**WALK 13**

A fine park for a relaxing wander. Like most Royal Parks this was once private hunting grounds for kings and queens. Now it hosts every possible activity, although hunting and duelling are no longer tolerated. Choose a pleasant day for this walk since you have only the trees for shelter.

**Start:** Marble Arch

**Finish:** High Street Kensington

**Distance:** 3 miles (4.7km)

**Refreshments:** The Orangery, Kensington Palace

Kensington Palace

## ON THIS WALK

Marble Arch | Hyde Park | Peter Pan
Speakers' Corner | Italian Gardens | Kensington Gardens

78 / WALK 13 – HYDE PARK

**Leave Marble Arch station by the Bayswater Road exit.**

Looking back you see **Oxford Street**, London's major shopping street with several flagship stores.

The **Marble Arch**, John Nash's memorial to the defeat of Napoleon, stood outside Buckingham Palace until 1851, but when it was found to be too narrow for the grandest carriages it was moved here.

This is the site of **Tyburn Tree**, the principle place of public execution in London from 1388 to 1783. Hanging days were public holidays and there was noisy support for a brave, dignified or theatrical death. Many of the doomed dressed themselves well and shaved on the morning of their death; flowers were strewn in the way of popular criminals; friends and relatives pulled on the legs to break their necks and help them die quickly. When the body was cut down some thought it held medicinal qualities and brushed the dead hand against their cheek.

Highwaymen were never the romantic figures of popular imagination apart from perhaps the glamorous Frenchman, **Claude Duval**. He invited lady victims to dance in the moonlight as he robbed them. His hanging at Tyburn was the scene of much loud lamentation from the sympathetic crowd in attendance, which allegedly included several masked ladies of quality. His body was cut down and he was given a lavish funeral at St Paul's. His epitaph says, 'Here lies Duval, Reader, if male thou art, Look to thy purse; if female look to thy heart'.

Look beyond Marble Arch to the corner of the park. The paved area is **Speakers' Corner**. By the 19th century Hyde Park had become a popular place for meetings and demonstrations, some of which deteriorated into rioting, so Speakers' Corner was established to create a venue where people would be allowed to speak freely. Here, every Sunday, anyone can stand on a soap box and pontificate on political, religious or other subjects, often barracked and challenged by their audience.

## Walk along the right-hand side of Bayswater Road.

In 1888, the American **George Train** created England's first horse-drawn tramway along the Bayswater Road – however wheels of hackney carriages buckled when they crashed against the tram lines. Vested interests who owned the cab firms proved too influential for the inaptly named Train and the trams were banned.

Pass **Tyburn Convent** on the right. It was founded in 1903 by the Adorers of the Sacred Heart of Jesus of Montmartre to pray for the souls of Roman Catholic martyrs who were hanged or burnt here. The Blessed Oliver Plunkett was the last English martyr, in 1681.

The red-brick **Oranjehaven** was established in 1942 by Queen Wilhelmina as a club for Dutch servicemen who'd escaped to fight with the Allied Forces against Hitler.

WALK 13 – HYDE PARK

**Cross the road at Albion Gate, enter the park and turn right along North Carriage Drive.**

You are now in **Hyde Park**, largest of the London parks: so large you could fit the entire City of London in it. In 1536, King Henry VIII confiscated this land from the monks of Westminster Abbey and used it for hunting. King Charles I opened the park to the public in 1637, then during the English Civil War the Parliamentary Army built fortifications against the Royalists. It remained popular for healthy active pursuits from 1649-1660 when England was a republic. The Lord Protector Oliver Cromwell, keen exponent of the wholesome sport of carriage racing, was tipped from his carriage and dragged along by the horses. A pistol went off in his pocket, but at last he got his foot clear and he survived, almost unscathed.

At the Restoration Charles II took the park back into Royal hands, built a high brick wall and restocked it with deer.

**Continue along North Carriage Drive to Victoria Gate.**

Enthusiastic riders can hire horses from the mews north of Bayswater Road; for others, take your pick - football, softball, jog, swim, row, picnic.

During the late 18th century, the park became a popular venue for duels. If a gentleman felt he had been

80 / WALK 13 – HYDE PARK

insulted, he might 'call the offender out'. Weapons were chosen and seconds appointed. During the 59-year reign of George III over 172 duels were recorded, accounting for 69 deaths and 96 seriously wounded. They were governed by a set of informal rules that set out a table of 26 insults (to family, manhood, conduct unbecoming a gentleman, etc.) that any self-respecting gentleman should not allow to pass and which outlined the responsibilities of the protagonists' seconds. The Duke of Wellington famously fought a duel as did the 18th-century Whig politician, Charles James Fox. He fought a Mr Adam here in 1779. When his second suggested he stand sideways on to minimise the target for his opponent's pistol, the corpulent Fox refused, spluttering 'Why man, I'm as thick one way as the other!'.

Through the bushes to the left of Victoria Lodge Gate is a **Pets' Cemetery**. First to be buried was Cherry, a Maltese Terrier, in 1881. More than 300 dogs, cats, canaries, etc. joined her until 1903 when it was declared full.

## Continue to Marlborough Gate.

Hyde Park has hosted large-scale free entertainments ever since Pink Floyd and Fleetwood Mac played here in 1968. Audiences of up to 80,000 have seen everyone from Luciano Pavarotti to Madonna. On the 'Last Night of the Proms' an alternative programme is presented here for the thousands unable to get tickets to the Albert Hall.

## Turn left at Marlborough Gate and with the water on your left walk alongside The Long Water.

The **Italian Gardens** were laid out in 1862 although the River Westbourne was dammed much earlier when

WALK 13 – HYDE PARK / 81

George II's wife Queen Caroline created The Long Water and Serpentine. Two yachts were put in the water for the Royal Family's use and the park was re-opened to a contingent of 'respectably dressed' folk.

## We are no longer in Hyde Park, but Kensington Gardens.

George Frampton's bronze statue of **Peter Pan** stands on the spot where Peter landed when he flew out of his nursery in his first adventure 'The Little White Bird'. J M Barrie lived close by on Bayswater Road and developed his world of Wendy, Captain Hook and the Lost Boys while entertaining the sons of the Llewelyn Davies family in Kensington Gardens. The sculptor shows Peter surrounded by fairies and rabbits. Perhaps birds would be more appropriate, as Kensington Gardens has comprehensive records of its wild birds that date back more than a hundred years. Not so for rabbits and fairies.

## Stop at the bridge.

The bridge divides The Long Water from **The Serpentine**, one of the earliest artificial lakes designed to appear natural. The lake achieved notoriety in December 1816 when Harriet, the pregnant wife of poet Percy Bysshe Shelley, was found drowned having left a suicide note. Shelley married Mary Godwin less than two weeks later.

The Serpentine Swimming Club is open all the year round. Due to the hazards of freezing water, 'The Peter Pan Christmas Day Race' is only open to regular winter swimmers.

In the 2012 London Olympics the swimming leg of the triathlon was held here before the cycling and running legs took the athletes all round Hyde Park.

## Do not cross the bridge but continue with The Serpentine on your left.

**The Diana, Princess of Wales Memorial Fountain** resembles an artificial stream rather than a fountain and was opened by Elizabeth II in 2004.

## Leave the fountain and turn right along the dirt track.

**Rotten Row** is a bridle path. King William III's chronic asthma was made worse by living on the river at Whitehall Palace and Queen Mary complained that she could see nothing but water or wall, so in 1689 they planned a move to Kensington Palace. At the time Hyde Park, although still officially private, was notorious for its footpads, highwaymen and ruffians. The king found the walk from Kensington Palace to Westminster rather intimidating, so 300 oil lamps were hung from trees along the Route du Roi. It wasn't long before this French phrase had been corrupted by Londoners into 'Rotten Row'.

## At West Carriage Drive turn left to Alexandra Gate.

Glance to the right towards the **Serpentine Gallery** with exhibitions of contemporary art.

## Just before Alexandra Gate turn right.

Across Kensington Gore is the **Royal Geographical Society** which contains the largest private collection of maps in the world and has sponsored and promoted many explorers. On its walls are statues of David Livingstone and Ernest Shackleton. Because one explored Africa and the other

Antarctica, this is known by cabbies as 'Hot and Cold Corner'.

The **Albert Memorial** is Queen Victoria's personal tribute to her beloved husband who died in 1861 aged 42. Albert was an intelligent, cultured German who craved more influence than he was allowed by parliament. To keep him out of politics he was encouraged to concentrate on education and the arts. He masterminded the 1851 **Great Exhibition** which attracted 6 million visitors to Hyde Park. Joseph Paxton's Crystal Palace displayed treasures from across the British Empire and Thomas Cook kick-started his travel business with cheap railway excursions from as far afield as Liverpool and Nottingham. The revenue raised went straight to Victoria, who used it to create 'Albertopolis', the impressive complex of museums in South Kensington.

Across the road is the **Royal Albert Hall**, home of the BBC Promenade Concerts which run from July to September and provide daily music at affordable prices. It is also used for individual concerts, boxing and tennis.

**Take Lancaster Walk directly away from the road and at Physical Energy turn left towards the Round Pond.**

The **Round Pond** is a pleasant place to pause for five minutes or so. Once there were formal Dutch Gardens here and a rectangular pond. During the 18th century the fashion for natural landscaping meant a gradual relaxation of style.

**Make your way across the Broad Walk to Kensington Palace.**

**Kensington Palace** has a chequered history. In the early 1700s Queen Anne introduced an orangery and gardens within the walls. King George I, who hated London and never learnt English, liked it because it reminded him of his palace at Herrenhausen Castle. His grandson George III passed it to his fourth son the Duke of Kent, whose daughter Victoria was born here in 1819. She lived in the palace until she became queen at 18.

Its associations with princesses continued as the late Queen's sister, Margaret, lived here until it became the home of Prince Charles and Princess Diana. After their divorce Diana retained an apartment until her sudden death in August 1997. The unprecedented outpouring of grief brought the Palace to the notice of the world as over an acre (4,000 square metres) of flowers were laid outside the gates.

**If you don't want to take refreshment in the Orangery follow the Broad Walk and bear diagonally right to Kensington High Street.**

Next to the Royal Garden hotel is a private road patrolled by armed police. **Kensington Palace Gardens** is the most expensive road in town with houses changing hands for over £100 million. Take a detour up it if you wish to see the former home of Bernie Ecclestone of Formula One and the Israeli and Russian Embassies, but be warned - no photography is allowed.

In **Kensington High Street**, the two great art deco department stores, Derry and Toms and Barker's, dominate. Nowadays they house independent shops and cafés. Take your pick.

# IN THE FOOTSTEPS OF THE SLOANE RANGER

# Chelsea

**WALK 14**

The Royal Borough of Kensington and Chelsea is so named because Queen Victoria was born in Kensington Palace. Always fashionable, arty and chic, Chelsea's first residents set the tone when wealthy families moved this side of London, where the air was clean and pasture good back in the days of Henry VIII.

| Start | Finish | Distance | Refreshments |
|---|---|---|---|
| Knightsbridge | Sloane Square | 3¼ miles (5.2km) | Peter Jones Espresso Bar |

*Peter Jones: the first glass curtain wall in London*

## ON THIS WALK

- Designer shops
- Sir Hans Sloane
- Oscar Wilde
- King's Road
- Saatchi Gallery
- The Royal Hospital

WALK 14 – CHELSEA

## Emerge from Knightsbridge Station.

Avoid being swept along by groups high-tailing it to **Harrods** in Knightsbridge to your left. Charles Henry Harrod, a tea merchant from Eastcheap, headed west to capitalise on the Great Exhibition of 1851 in nearby Hyde Park. Now the imposing terracotta department store is the most famous shop in London with its motto 'Everything for Everybody Everywhere'. Here customers could use the first escalators in London: to steady the nerves a young man stood at the top with brandy for gentlemen and smelling salts for the ladies.

## Walk down Sloane Street.

**Harvey Nichols** is to your left. This vivid and exciting store with designer collections was much loved in the 1980s by wealthy, fashionable young women, known as Sloane Rangers. The store might even open an hour or so late on mornings when Diana, Princess of Wales was given the space for private shopping.

The **designer shops** on both sides of the road don't make enough in sales to pay the ground rent. They are here to expose the label in the right place. One month you may window shop at Dior and Bulgari; next month it might be Gucci, Hermes or Cartier.

Glance down the streets to your right as you walk and you will see into 'Hans Town' a grand suburb named after **Sir Hans Sloane**. As a young man in the late 1600s Sloane became personal physician to the Governor of Jamaica, where he was introduced to a drink called cocoa. He found it 'nauseous' but by mixing it with hot milk and sugar he invented a chocolate recipe later taken up by Messrs Cadbury. Sloane was an avid collector and on his death aged 93 the government bought his 71,000 natural history specimens, coins and books for £20,000. This provided the core collection for the new 'British Museum'.

One of Sloane's daughters married Lord Cadogan and doubled both families' lands. The Cadogan Hotel stands on the corner of the square that should rightly be called a rectangle. It was here in 1895 that **Oscar Wilde** was arrested for 'gross indecency'. John Betjeman's poem captures the moment, 'Mr Wilde, we've come for to take you/ Where felons and criminals dwell/ We ask you to come with us quietly/ For this is the Cadogan Hotel'.

At the same time the actress **Lily Langtry** was in residence next door where she installed a new-fangled machine for printing out updated racing results.

**Holy Trinity Church** on the left is according to Betjeman 'The Cathedral of the Arts and Crafts Movement' whose aim was to make everyday things beautiful and to revere Nature through crafts, painting and sculpture. Do explore inside. The nave is wider than that of St Paul's Cathedral and round every corner is finely crafted work by

| National Army Museum | | Cheyne Walk | | Mary Quant |
|---|---|---|---|---|
| | Chelsea Physic Garden | | The Chelsea Potter | | Thomas Crapper |

WALK 14 – CHELSEA

the likes of William Morris and Edward Burne Jones.

## Turn right into Sloane Square.

**The Royal Court Theatre** is considered the home of new British drama. In the 1950s George Devine aimed to create a writers' theatre, where the play was more important than actors, director, or designer. John Osborne's Look Back in Anger shocked audiences in 1956. The curtain opened on a dingy bed-sit with a young woman in her slip ironing, while her husband ranted about the complacency of the wartime generation and the state of Britain. The Royal Court Publicity Officer said that Osborne was an 'Angry Young Man' which struck a chord and the play began to attract a new audience, younger than the traditional West End clientele.

**Peter Jones** department store was founded in 1877. After Jones's death in 1905, the business foundered, but John Lewis walked from his own Oxford Street store with £20,000 in cash in his pocket to buy the company. In the 1930s the first glass curtain wall in London was erected and architects recently voted it one of the most important buildings of the 20th century.

## Walk along the King's Road to Royal Avenue.

**King's Road** was developed in the late 17th century as a private road for Charles II between Hampton Court and Westminster. Until 1830 only those who had been issued with an official copper pass marked 'King's Private Road' could use it. Subsequently it became the most bohemian part of London, culminating in its apotheosis as a fashionable promenading route in the 1960s.

**Duke of York's Square** to the left was sold by the Territorial Army for £66 million in 2000 to be redeveloped into a shopping square. Charles Saatchi who, with his brother Maurice, created the largest advertising agency group in the world established **The Saatchi Gallery** here. In the 1990s Saatchi was responsible for building the public profiles of Young British Artists such as Damien Hirst and Tracey Emin. Many of his new acquisitions are on display along with visiting exhibitions.

**Whitelands House** on the corner with Cheltenham Terrace is the former base for Oswald Mosley's British Union of Fascists in the 1930s. It was known back then as 'The Black House' after the colour of their shirts.

## Turn left down Royal Avenue.

**Royal Avenue** and Burton Court are part of Sir Christopher Wren's and Charles II's grand scheme to link the Royal Hospital with Kensington Palace. The death of the king meant it was never completed. Although Wren laid the square out in the 1600s, the houses date from 250 years later. It is the fictional home of James Bond.

## Turn left along St Leonard's Terrace, right down Franklin's Row and right along Royal Hospital Road.

Wren's first public commission had been **The Royal Hospital Chelsea** as a home for old soldiers and inspired by Les Invalides in Paris. Chelsea Pensioners must be over 65 and in receipt of an Army Service or War Disability Pension. When they are out and about they wear their distinctive scarlet coats and medals. In 2009 the first two female pensioners were admitted.

Every May the Royal Horticultural Society holds the **Chelsea Flower Show** in the grounds which heralds the beginning of the social 'season' – Glorious Goodwood, the Henley Regatta, tennis at Wimbledon and the Lord's Test Match.

**The National Army Museum** was founded in 1960 by Field Marshal Templer who took control of the government in Malaya during the communist insurgency in 1952, coining the phrase 'winning the hearts and minds'. Inside is a fine art gallery, the skeleton of Napoleon's horse Marengo, lace from a coat belonging to King William III, kit and belongings of the ordinary soldiers over the centuries, not to mention a section of the Berlin Wall.

## Cross Tite Street and continue.

The American artist **James McNeil Whistler**, who lived in Tite Street in

WALK 14 – CHELSEA / 87

*The Chelsea Potter*

and in 1722 Sir Hans Sloane gave them the freehold. They introduced the use of a stove under the conservatory to preserve tender herbs and plants through the coldest winter, established the earliest rock garden in England and as well as herbs and medicinal plants, grew trees and shrubs from all over the world, including the largest olive tree in England.

### Continue along Cheyne Walk to Beaufort Street.

There are so many blue plaques and associations along the fashionable length of **Cheyne Walk** (pronounced 'chainy'). The artist J M W Turner spent his last 7 years here living incognito as 'Mr Booth'. Dante Gabriel Rossetti, Elizabeth Gaskell, George Eliot and the man who Dickens called The Sage of Chelsea, Thomas Carlyle. Carlyle didn't suffer fools gladly and the novelist Samuel Butler said, 'It was very good of God to let Carlyle and Mrs Carlyle marry one another and so make only two people miserable instead of four'.

There is no plaque to the police dawn raid on the home of Mick Jagger and Marianne Faithful or where Keith Richards and Anita Pallenberg were also raided by the Drug Squad and fined £275 in 1973.

Look ahead at the **Albert Bridge**, painted a delicate pink and blue, like a birthday cake for a little girl with ringlets and a lisp. Built in 1873 to ease

the second half of the 19th century, was an archetypal Chelsea character. He became known as the 'The King of Chelsea' and his abstract style shocked contemporaries. The critic John Ruskin wrote 'I never expected to hear a coxcomb ask two hundred guineas for flinging a pot of paint in the public's face.' The artist sued Ruskin for libel. In court Whistler was asked if he thought the two days' labour on a painting was worth that much: "No," he replied, "I ask it for the knowledge of a lifetime." Everyone applauded! Whistler won and Ruskin resigned his post at Oxford. But the damages amounted to a farthing leaving the artist, after costs, financially devastated.

**The Chelsea Physic Garden** was established by the Society of Apothecaries in 1676 on land ideal for growing herbs and medicinal plants,

the traffic load on Battersea Bridge, it became unstable in the 1950s. John Betjeman led the battle to save it from demolition. It still has the sign warning troops to break step.

Across the river is **Battersea Park** with its Buddhist Peace Pagoda built by Japanese monks in 1986.

**Roper's Garden** is named after Margaret Roper, the daughter of Sir Thomas More. He it was who began the fashion for building here in 1520, partly for the clean air and countryside but no doubt with half an eye on the political capital gained from being close to the King at Hampton Court.

On the corner of Danvers Street is **Crosby Hall** which originally stood on the other side of London in Bishopsgate. Allegedly the home of Richard III before he became King, it was moved here brick by brick in 1907 to become the Federation of University Women. It was bought by a private owner in the 1980s and is no longer open to the public.

## Turn right up Beaufort Street.

On the site of Thomas More's 16th-century 'Great House' is **Allen Hall**, the Catholic Seminary of the Archdiocese of Westminster. Founded in exile in northern France in 1568, its former students include the most renowned of English martyrs, Thomas Campion, in whose honour many catholic schools are named.

## Turn right and walk straight along the King's Road back to Sloane Square.

If at any point your legs feel weary, you'll find somewhere to stop for refreshment.

At **Chelsea Old Town Hall**, Judy Garland married her 5th husband Micky Deans. Only 50 people turned up: within months she was dead from an overdose of drugs.

**The Chelsea Potter** is still here: once the local for struggling young flat mates, Michael Caine and Terence Stamp, so poor that they had to share a smart jacket for auditions.

As its name suggests, the stylish 19th-century **Pheasantry**, now Pizza Express, was a shop which sold pheasants. From 1916 the ballerina Princess Seraphina Astafieva, great-niece of Leo Tolstoy, taught many aspiring young dancers including Alice Marks and Peggy Hookham; these two later found fame as Alicia Markova and Margot Fonteyn.

In 1955 **Mary Quant** opened the country's first boutique, Bazaar, at 138a. She introduced 'The Look' and created the 'Dolly Bird' – floppy hats, skinny rib sweaters and the mini skirt with white Courreges boots.

Subsequent hippy enclaves like 'Gandalf's Bric-a-brac Shop' and 'Granny Takes a Trip' have also disappeared in a puff of smoke.

Down **Bywater Street** another fictional spy, George Smiley, lived unhappily with, or more often than not without, his wife.

At No. 120 **Thomas Crapper**, the Royal Plumber, had his flagship store. He patented the flushing lavatory and invented the bathroom showroom. His displays behind large plate glass windows caused a stir and it is said that ladies observing the china bowls in the windows became faint at this shocking sight!

Between here and Sloane Square there is a rich variety of cafés, bars and restaurants, or if you prefer, in the great tradition of the King's Road, promenade like a 'dedicated follower of fashion'.

# TURN AGAIN WHITTINGTON

# Highgate

**WALK 15**

Travellers and drovers were required to pay a toll to a hermit at the High Gate to pass through the Bishop of London's hunting park. Its fresh air, fine views and clean spring water encouraged many to move here over the past 500 years and it remains one of the most sought after residential communities in London.

| **Start** | **Finish** | **Distance** | **Refreshments** |
|---|---|---|---|
| Highgate | Archway | 2½ miles (3.9km) | Characterful pubs and teashops in Highgate village |

Highgate School

## ON THIS WALK

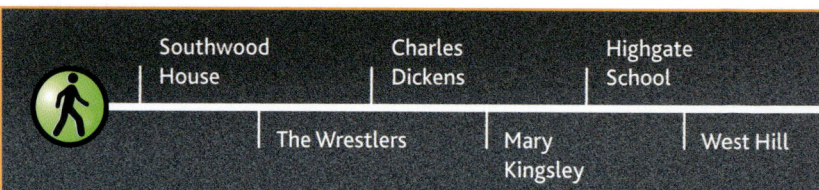

- Southwood House
- The Wrestlers
- Charles Dickens
- Mary Kingsley
- Highgate School
- West Hill

🚶 Leave the station, cross Archway Road and walk up Jackson's Lane. The road is narrow, be careful.

**Jacksons Lane Arts Centre** was once Highgate Methodist Church. Bank Point and Hillside are two 18th-century houses, delightful but utterly different.

### At the junction with Southwood Lane turn right up Park Walk.

**Southwood House** stood on your left where the red-brick apartment block Southwood Park now stands. It was the home of General Wade who between the Jacobite Risings of 1715 and 1745 was 'Commander in Chief of His Majesty's forces, castles, forts and barracks in North Britain'. In this role he constructed some 250 miles (400 km) of road, plus 40 bridges (including the ill-fated Tay Bridge). His fame was such that he had a verse to himself in the new National Anthem: 'Lord, grant that Marshal Wade/ May, by thy mighty aid/ Victory bring. / May he sedition hush/ And like a torrent rush/ Rebellious Scots to crush, / God save the King'.

This verse is rarely sung nowadays.

### Turn left at the end of Park Walk along North Road.

**The Wrestlers** started life in 1547 and is one of the Highgate pubs privy to the ceremony of 'Swearing on the Horns'. This apparently dates back to 1635 when a pair of stag's horns on a stick would be placed in front of an innocent traveller while the landlord recited a series of nonsensical conditions – 'you must not drink small beer when you can drink strong; you must not kiss the maid when you can kiss the mistress, unless you like the maid best, etc.' Its purpose is lost in the mists of time, but one assumes it usually ended with the victim making a mistake and being 'encouraged' to buy drink for the locals. The Wrestlers still conducts this ceremony twice a year.

The plaque to **Charles Dickens** at No. 92 commemorates the time when his father brought the family to Highgate to avoid his creditors. Charles at 20 was working as a court reporter at the time and was on the verge of being published.

Highgate is a showcase for English residential styles of architecture, with nothing more influential than Berthold Lubetkin's 1930s **'High Point'** apartments across the road. These heralded the arrival of a European style of living in communal blocks. Lubetkin came from the Soviet Union via Germany and championed modern materials like concrete, flexible living spaces, roof gardens and use of natural light. Highpoint One was commissioned by Sigmund Gestetner, head of the office equipment firm, as social housing for his workers and Lubetkin was given free rein to develop his ideas. They are considered a fine example of 'modernism', are 'Grade One Listed' and may not be tinkered with.

| Sir Francis Bacon | Dick Whittington | | Angela Burdett Coutts | |
|---|---|---|---|---|
| | | Pond Square | The West Cemetery | The East Cemetery |

### Turn left down Castle Yard and right along Southwood Lane.

**Arthur Waley**, orientalist and translator of 'The Pillow Book of Sei Shonagon' and 'Monkey' lived at No. 50.

On the right are **Almshouses** originally built by Sir John Wollaston, a London goldsmith, in the 1600s as dwellings for the poor. They were reconstructed in 1726 by Edward Pauncefort, with a charity school for 24 girls in the middle.

The explorer **Mary Kingsley** grew up over the road in No. 22, Avalon. Her father travelled the world while Mary had to stay at home and care for her invalid mother. The windows were bricked up, not because of Window Tax but so that Mrs Kingsley could have peace and quiet. Both parents died when Mary was 29 and she determined to finish her father's book on the culture of Africa. She learnt fishing and hunting skills in Angola and set off into the mangrove swamps to collect specimens of unknown fish for the British Museum. Her canoe was attacked by a crocodile and she encountered head-hunters. In 1897 her book 'Travels in West Africa' became a bestseller but subsequent articles upset the Church of England when she openly criticised missionaries for trying to change the West Africans' way of life.

Across the roundabout at Highgate Hill, **The Gatehouse** pub stands where the Tollgate once was. Years after the death of the last hermit, Turnpike Trusts were introduced. From the 18th century toll money went to the local council who were responsible for maintaining the roads. By 1826 there were 19 taverns in Highgate and 80 coaches passed through the toll each day. Too high for a railway line, Highgate became quieter until the arrival of the motor car and now even though Archway Road by-passes the village the traffic never stops.

### Turn right and duck down North Road for a few metres.

**Highgate School** has a strong music tradition. Composers John Rutter and John Taverner were both pupils. It was founded in 1565 as a 'grammar school for good education and instruction'. In 1916 a ten-year old John Betjeman presented his teacher Mr T S Eliot with a handwritten collection of poems called 'The Best of Betjeman'. Even years later, Eliot would never tell him what he thought of them.

Opposite at No. 10 North Road the poet **A E Housman** wrote much of his long poem 'A Shropshire Lad', a wistful evocation of doomed youth in the English countryside.

### Turn into Hampstead Lane and then go left to walk down the right-hand side of The Grove.

**Fitzroy Park** on the right leads to an exclusive estate reputedly laid out in the 1770s by the landscape gardener 'Capability' Brown.

**The Grove** was originally developed by a city merchant in 1688 as three pairs of semi-detached properties. Although added to since, it retains a unique character.

In the 1930s **Robert Donat**, who Charles Laughton called 'the most graceful actor of our time', lived at No. 8. He won the Oscar in 1939 for 'Goodbye, Mr Chips', beating Clark Gable, Laurence Olivier, Mickey Rooney and James Stewart.

At No. 3 the poet **Samuel Taylor Coleridge** spent his last years in the

care of Dr Gillman and his family. **J B Priestley**, playwright and novelist, also lived here from 1931 to 1945. During World War II his down-to-earth radio 'postscripts' acted as a homely balance to Churchill's oratory: Falstaff to the Prime Minister's Henry V. A more recent resident was George Michael who died on Christmas Day 2016.

The violin virtuoso **Yehudi Menuhin** once lived at No. 2.

The arched gatehouse of **Witanhurst**, built for a soap manufacturer in 1913, stands at the top of the hill. It is reckoned the second largest private house in London after Buckingham Palace, sits in six acres (2.4 hectares) of woodland and has some of the finest views of London. It was bought in 2008 for around £70 million by an offshore company rumoured to be acting for the richest woman in Russia, wife of a former Mayor of Moscow. She denies it.

See how steep **West Hill** is. In 1837, John Turner, landlord of The Fox Under the Hill, saw an out of control carriage and four careering down the hill. He

WALK 15 – HIGHGATE / 93

blocked the wheels with an iron bar and stopped the horses. One of the passengers was the young, still to be crowned queen, **Victoria**. For saving her life – and changing history – he was given a Royal Coat of Arms for the wall of his pub and the honour of changing its name to The Fox and Crown.

## Cross the road and walk left along South Grove to Pond Square.

On the left is **The Flask**, an unpretentious late 18th-century pub, with an extensive beer garden and cosy bars.

Built in 1831 **St Michael's Church** replaced the Bishop of London's 12th-century Chantry. It is the highest parish church in London. Poet Samuel Taylor Coleridge's body was moved from a local graveyard in 1961 and re-interred in the crypt here. Poet Laureate John Masefield gave the address and Coleridge's own words are his epitaph. 'Stop, passer-by, stop Child of God and read with gentle breast. Beneath the sod a poet lies, or that which once seemed he, O lift one thought in prayer to STC'.

No. 17 **Old Hall**, home of the actress Margaret Rutherford for many years, was built in 1691 on the site of Arundel House. **Sir Francis Bacon** died here. Occasionally cited as the man who wrote Shakespeare's plays he deserves to be remembered as the 'Father of Modern Science'. Until Bacon, scientific advances were decided by argument in the style of Aristotle: he championed the use of experiment. It was here in 1626 it occurred to him that ice might preserve food as effectively as salt. He bought, plucked and eviscerated a chicken then stuffed it with snow. His observations took so long that he caught a chill, was given a bed at the Earl of Arundel's house: the bed had not been aired properly and according to the gossip, John Aubrey, it 'gave him such a cold that in 2 or 3 days, as I remember, he died.'

In 2001 the architects Eldridge Smerin 'wrapped' **The Lawns**, a 1950s detached house in glass, doubling its area but retaining the original features. It was seen as an exemplar of how to build a 21st-century house in a conservation area.

Although set slightly back, the 19th-century **Union Chapel** rather jars with the older houses in the street.

**Pond Square**. The succession of hermits charged with collecting tolls dug gravel to repair pot holes in the road. The resulting 'ponds' eventually became stagnant and had to be filled in.

In 'David Copperfield' Dickens gave Steerforth's wealthy mother an 'old brick house in Highgate on the very summit of the hill', believed to be No. 10, **Church House**.

Next door, the **Highgate Literary and Scientific Institution** was founded in 1839 and still provides libraries, lectures and courses.

## Turn right down Highgate Hill.

This is **Highgate village**. It bravely tries to maintain its charm in the face of constant traffic and you can see by the number of yards behind existing shops where inns like The Duke's Head would once have stood.

As **Dick Whittington** began to trudge up Highgate Hill with his cat, he heard the bells of St Mary le Bow say, 'Turn again Whittington, Lord Mayor of London'. Would that this was true. Whittington was in fact a smart businessman and Lord Mayor of London four times. He gave Henry V money to fight the French at Agincourt and in return got the sole right to sell coal in the city.

## Go through the gates of Waterlow Park on your right.

The Holly Estate, Swain's Lane

As well as creating this splendid park in 1889 as 'a garden for the gardenless' the Victorian philanthropist **Sydney Waterlow** provided over 30,000 working people with 'healthy, commodious and cheap dwellings' across London through his Industrial Dwellings Company.

## Walk through the park past the tennis courts and bend right with the path to emerge on Swain's Lane. Turn left down the hill.

To your right, the gates of **The West Cemetery**. London expanded in the early years of the 19th century and seven new cemeteries were commissioned. Highgate's was set out and opened in 1839. The burials here encompass Michael Faraday, the electricity pioneer, the wife and parents of Charles Dickens and the novelist Beryl Bainbridge. The only access to the West Cemetery is as part of a pre-booked tour which takes place each lunchtime.

The mock Tudor **Holly Estate** to your right was the brainchild of perhaps the greatest of our philanthropists, **Angela Burdett Coutts**. She inherited half of Coutts Bank in 1837 at the age of 23 and became Britain's richest woman save the Queen. She also inherited the country house at The Holly Lodge and formed the 'Lady Workers' Homes Limited' to build blocks of rooms for single women who'd moved to London to work as secretaries and clerks in the city. It remains a unique gated community owned by its 'plot-holders'.

In her lifetime, Angela gave away between £3 and £4 million pounds on good works. She established the NSPCC and the RSPCA, set up soup kitchens, provided cotton gins for Nigeria, poured money into the fishing industry and agriculture of Ireland after the famine, built homes for fallen women to learn sewing and weaving skills, found placements in the Royal Navy for destitute boys, and even established drinking fountains for dogs in parks throughout the country.

Much of her early work was in cahoots with Charles Dickens but they fell out when he left his wife and ten children for a young actress. They were never reconciled. Before she died aged 92 she became the first woman to be made a Baroness in her own right and the Prince of Wales praised her as the second greatest woman in the kingdom.

## Turn left off Swain's Lane and walk along Chester Road.

On the left are the gates of **The East Cemetery**. You are free to explore this part of the cemetery – there is an entry fee and a map is provided. The most famous tomb is that of Karl Marx but don't forget George Eliot, Henry Moore, Douglas Adams and many more. The roll call is on a par with Père Lachaise in Paris.

For Archway, the nearest station, head for the Whittington Hospital on Highgate Hill and turn right. Otherwise it's back up the hill to one of the characterful pubs or tea shops in Highgate village.

For Maggie.

| | |
|---|---|
| **Walks:** | Devised and written by Andy Rashleigh |
| **Photography:** | Andy Rashleigh. Cover: © Samot, Shutterstock; page 76, Eluveitie via Wikimedia Commons |
| **Maps:** | Cosmographics Ltd |
| **Design:** | Ark Creative (UK) Ltd |

© Crown copyright / Ordnance Survey Limited, 2024
Published by Milestone Publishing Ltd under licence from Ordnance Survey Limited. Pathfinder, Ordnance Survey, OS and the OS logos are registered trademarks of Ordnance Survey Limited and are used under licence from Ordnance Survey Limited.
Text © Milestone Publishing Limited, 2024

The right of Andy Rashleigh to be identified as the author of this work has been asserted by him in accordance with the Copyright, Designs and Patents Act, 1988.

ISBN: 978-0-31909-035-0

This product includes mapping data licensed from Ordnance Survey
© Crown copyright and database rights (2024) OS AC0000819511.

All rights reserved. No part of this publication may be reproduced, transmitted in any form or by any means, or stored in a retrieval system without either the prior written permission of the publisher, or in the case of reprographic reproduction a licence issued in accordance with the terms and licences issued by the CLA Ltd.

While every care has been taken to check the accuracy and reliability of the information in this guide, the author and publisher cannot accept responsibility for errors or omissions or for changes in details given. When walking in London it is advisable at all times to act with due care and attention, and anyone using this guide is responsible for their own well-being and safety.

First published in Great Britain 2012 by Crimson Publishing and reprinted with amendments in 2017.

First published 2020 by Trotman Publishing.

This edition first published 2022 by Milestone Publishing.
Reprinted with amendments 2024.

Milestone Publishing, 19-21D Charles Street, Bath, BA1 1HX
pathfinderwalks.co.uk

Printed in India by Replika Press Pvt. Ltd. 5/24

A catalogue record for this book is available from the British Library.

Front cover: St Paul's Cathedral
Title page: Red telephone boxes